MANAGING UPWARD

Strategies for Succeeding with Your Boss

Patti Hathaway
and Susan D. Schubert

A FIFTY-MINUTE™ SERIES BOOK

Viva Books Private Limited
New Delhi • Mumbai • Chennai • Kolkata • Bangalore • Hyderabad

First Indian Edition 2004
Reprinted 2005

VIVA BOOKS PRIVATE LIMITED

- 4262/3 Ansari Road, Daryaganj, New Delhi 110 002
  E-mail: viva@vivagroupindia.net
- 215-216 New Apollo Estate, 2nd Floor, Mogra Lane, Andheri (E), Mumbai 400 069 E-mail: vivamumbai@vivagroupindia.net
- Jamals Fazal Chambers, 26 Greams Road, Chennai 600 006
  E-mail: vivachennai@vivagroupindia.net
- B-103, Jindal Towers, 21/1A/3 Darga Road, Kolkata 700 017
  E-mail: vivakolkata@vivagroupindia.net
- 7 GF, Sovereign Park Apts., 56-58 K.R. Road, Basavanagudi, Bangalore 560 004 E-mail: vivabangalore@vivagroupindia.net
- 101 & 102, First Floor, Mughal Marg Apartments, Narayanaguda, Hyderabad 500 029 E-mail: vivahyderabad@vivagroupindia.net

Published by arrangement with

Crisp Publications, Inc.
1200 Hamilton Court,
Menlo Park
CA 94025
USA

Credits:
Editor: Kay Keppler
Designer: Carol Harris
Typesetting: ExecuStaff
Cover Design: Fifth Street Design and Amy Shayne
Artwork: Ralph Mapson

ISBN 81-7649-595-6

Published by Vinod Vasishtha for Viva Books Private Limited, 4262/3 Ansari Road, Daryaganj, New Delhi 110 002 and printed & bound at Raj Press, R-3 Inderpuri, New Delhi-110 012

LEARNING OBJECTIVES FOR:

MANAGING UPWARD

The objectives for *Managing Upward* are listed below. They have been developed to guide you, the reader, to the core issues covered in this book.

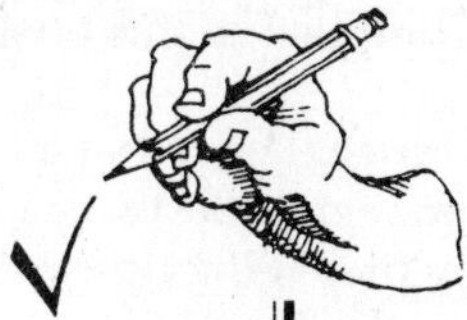

Objectives

- ❑ **1) To explain the characteristics of good employer-employee relationships**
- ❑ **2) To show how to communicate with a boss effectively**
- ❑ **3) To show how to identify types of leadership personalities**
- ❑ **4) To help solve employer-employee relationship problems**

Assessing Your Progress

In addition to the learning objectives, Crisp, Inc. has developed an **assessment** that covers the fundamental information presented in this book. A twenty-five item, multiple choice/true-false questionnaire allows the reader to evaluate his or her comprehension of the subject matter. An answer sheet with a chart matching the questions to the listed objectives is also available. To learn how to obtain a copy of this assessment, please call **1-800-442-7477** and ask to speak with a Customer Service Representative.

Assessments should not be used in any selection process.

PREFACE

As professional speakers and trainers, we are constantly asked for suggestions on how to manage more effectively. Regardless of geographical region, industry or profession, people want to know how they can be more productive and enhance their careers, in spite of, or with the help of, their bosses.

The ideas and strategies presented in this book come from the people who have attended our seminars and the organizations with which we have consulted. We have tested the concepts and exercises with employees who have tried them. Compiled in this book are ideas that work.

Our challenge to you is to not only read the book, but also experience the strategies. Best wishes to you as you begin the challenge of managing your career by managing upward!

Patty Hathaway — Susan Schubert

ACKNOWLEDGMENTS

Special thanks to:

Barbara Braham and Rita Milios for criticizing and editing the manuscript.

Elaine Fencl, Scott Ferguson, Susan Konves, Lindsey Lawrence, John E. Meighan, Ph.D. and Hal Merz for completing the exercises, trying out our strategies and providing feedback. Tamara L. Curry for sharing her techniques.

Columbus State Community College staff, Riverside Methodist Hospital staff and the Columbus Area Leadership Program graduates who participated in focus groups to talk about the strategies they used to manage their bosses and the strategies others used to manage them.

To all the supervisors and employees who appeared in disguise. Their identities shall never be revealed.

CONTENTS

SECTION I

Introduction

This Book Is for Everyone with a Boss

This book is written for everyone who works for someone else, including first-line supervisors, mid-level managers, secretaries and team leaders. The basic concepts are applicable in manufacturing, education, profit-driven and nonprofit organizations where teamwork between employees and their managers can benefit individuals, the total organization and, ultimately, its customers.

WHAT IS A BOSS?

Several words are used interchangeably to designate a person who receives direction, training, correction, etc., from another. These words include employee, direct report, staff.

The words boss, manager and supervisor mean those responsible by title and actions for leading, training and evaluating other people. Usually these people have a designated management position in the organization. However, they may assume supervisory roles in time-limited situations such as task forces, committees or when an employee "fills in" for a supervisor.

WHO MANAGES WHOM?

Employees share the responsibility for managing the relationship between themselves and their superiors. Exercised with skill and initiative rather than passivity and powerlessness, that role can strengthen everyone's motivation and productivity. Authors John J. Gabarro and John P. Kotter state that "managing upward" is the art of *consciously* improving collaboration with one's boss, to gain the best personal and organizational outcomes. It is not just superficial manipulating and empty praise. Alice Kelvin writes that many subordinates avoid upward managing because of prior experiences with authority figures. The role of employee seems like the passive early role of a child or student who unquestioningly accepts instruction from superiors—parents and teachers. By breaking the pattern of passivity, employees can become truly motivated, based on feelings of competence, self control and perceived results.

WHAT THIS BOOK WILL DO

This book will help you to improve your working arrangement with your boss, if you use the strategies outlined. Your positive actions will help you to:

- Clarify misunderstandings that obstruct the quality and quantity of your work
- Manage yourself better so you can be a role model for your boss and colleagues
- Take calculated risks
- Turn anger and frustration into constructive assertiveness
- Decide when the relationship is not manageable

BENEFITS

Rarely, if ever, are employees trained in techniques necessary for creating more effective collaboration with their supervisors. A solid professional relationship improves employees' job performances and their mental and physical health. If you master upward management techniques, you can achieve a number of personal and professional goals for yourself.

To obtain maximum results from this book, complete the exercises. Some you can do alone; others you must do with your supervisor. The exercises start with general, fairly easy questions and topics. They build on acquired skills, as you continue through the book, and end with complex situations based on actual circumstances.

WHY ARE YOU READING THIS BOOK?

Following is a list of potential outcomes from using the techniques in this book. Please check those benefits that you would like to experience.

Exercise 1: Benefits

_____ **1.** Reduce physical and mental stress

_____ **2.** Increase opportunity for recognition and promotion

_____ **3.** Implement ideas

_____ **4.** Increase self-confidence, motivation and morale

_____ **5.** Increase respect from colleagues

_____ **6.** Help make a career decision about whether to leave job

_____ **7.** Anticipate and avoid problems with my boss

_____ **8.** Improve the quality and quantity of my work

_____ **9.** Increase enjoyment of my job

_____ **10.** Other (specify) ________________________________

> *Concentrate* on your desired benefits as you take these important steps toward strengthening cooperative collaboration between yourself and your supervisor.

DEFINING THE PARTNERSHIP AND HOW IT CAN WORK BETTER

A satisfying relationship between a manager and employees may be compared to a successful partnership. People enter a partnership because they perceive that by combining their efforts and resources they can achieve their goals better than if they work solo. The manager and employee may have written documents such as a contract, job description, policies and procedures that specify their contributions—what each gives—and compensation—what each gets. However, a great part of working relationships is based on historical practices and unwritten assumptions. To improve the working partnership, vague assumptions must be converted into specific agreements. Typical examples of the contribution/compensation partnership follow.

CONTRIBUTION/COMPENSATION PARTNERSHIP

The Employer Gives	**The Employee Gives**
Security Appreciation Training Advice Money Tools and equipment to produce work	Time Knowledge Skills Dependability
The Employer Gets	**The Employee Gets**
Quality work Loyalty Commitment Dependability Recognition	Money Appreciation Challenge

THINK ABOUT YOUR SITUATION

Now think about your own working partnership. List two or three essential elements in your relationship with your boss. See if you can determine what your boss gets from you and gives to you. Then, complete both sides of the following equation.

Exercise 2: Compensation/Contribution Partnership

My Boss Gives Me	**I Give My Boss**
(Example: Opportunities for additional education.)	(Example: Specialized skills in solving engineering problems.)
______________________________	______________________________
______________________________	______________________________
______________________________	______________________________
______________________________	______________________________
______________________________	______________________________
______________________________	______________________________
______________________________	______________________________
______________________________	______________________________

My Boss Receives	**I Receive**
(Example: Work that is thorough and usually completed on time.)	(Example: Challenging work)
______________________________	______________________________
______________________________	______________________________
______________________________	______________________________
______________________________	______________________________
______________________________	______________________________
______________________________	______________________________
______________________________	______________________________
______________________________	______________________________

Exercise 3: Level of Understanding Between You and Your Supervisor

By completing these lists, you have begun to get a better understanding of your relationship with your boss. Now review your answers by responding to the following questions with "yes," "no," or "unsure."

__________ 1. Do you understand what your manager wants you to contribute to your relationship?

__________ 2. Do you receive equitable compensation—salary plus intangible appreciation, etc.—for the effort, knowledge, skills and abilities you contribute to the organization?

__________ 3. Does your supervisor know what you need from him or her to perform your work satisfactorily?

__________ 4. Do you think your boss believes s/he is receiving a fair exchange—commitment, results, etc.—from you?

__________ 5. Do you and your supervisor collectively agree that your partnership is beneficial for each of you?

Even if you answered "yes" to all of these questions, you can improve your work situation in many practical ways by applying upward management skills.

CLARIFY YOUR RELATIONSHIP

To obtain more clarification, you may wish to do one or more of the following:

- Review your latest performance evaluation to determine where you need to improve and see what your manager emphasizes

- Review job description, work plans, goals and objectives

- Talk to associates who may have ideas about how to improve communications with your mutual supervisor

- Hold a meeting with your boss

Once you have a better idea of the relationship you would like to have with your boss, it is time to look at what this relationship can do for both you and your organization.

SECTION

II

Focusing on the Big Picture

When organizations lack clear focus, they are less successful than they could be because they lack direction and purpose. Employees who lack clarity of focus and purpose find it difficult to achieve career success. An important key to an effective partnership between employees and managers is establishing team goals, priorities and plans to achieve those goals.

WHERE DO I START?

Most organizations hire employees to fit a job description and then tell them why they are there and what they should do. Employees function quite easily without their own personal goals and direction. However, personal goals can provide you with energy, enthusiasm and a clear plan on how to get things done in your job.* Unless you clarify how your personal goals are connected to organizational direction, you may become frustrated or burned out.

Blessing/White, a personal and corporate growth training company headquartered in Princeton, New Jersey, developed a career development program called Managing Personal Growth (MPG). MPG employs a model—modified here—to explain how an organization's goals and values intersect with an individual's goals and values to increase productivity and effectiveness.

The intersection in the middle of the model represents your job. If your organization or boss is very clear about the company's goals and values, then that will translate into clear expectations for you. The result is that the company will probably get what it wants from you: maximum productivity. But if the organization and manager are unfocused about their expectations and priorities, employees will be unclear about what to do and productivity will decline. Clear organizational goals and values provide employees with a sense of direction and mission.

*For an excellent resource on personal goals, read *Finding Your Purpose* by Barbara Braham (CRISP Publications, Inc.).

MPG Model

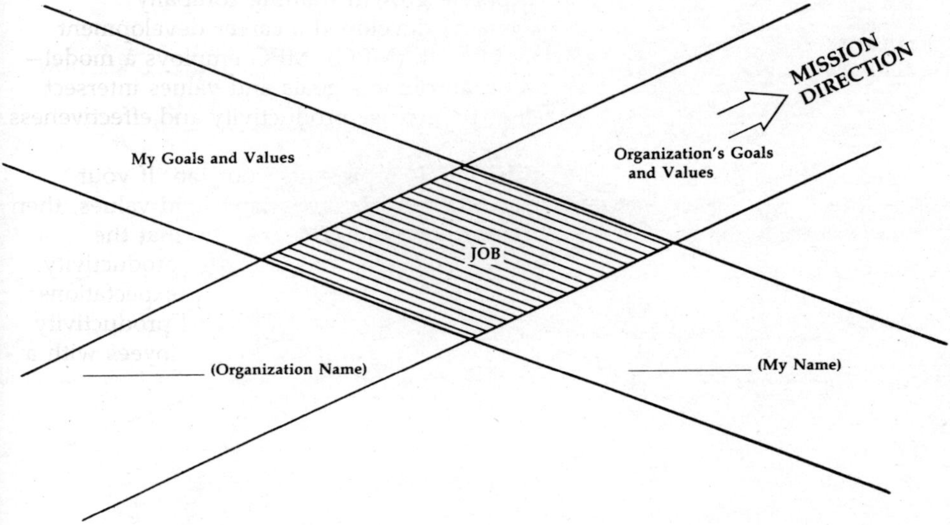
MISSION DIRECTION
My Goals and Values
Organization's Goals and Values
JOB
(Organization Name)
(My Name)

WHERE DO I START (continued)

You may be productive because the organization has defined its goals and expectations for you, yet you may not have defined what would make you happy or satisfied in that job. When you define your values, you gain energy and purpose.

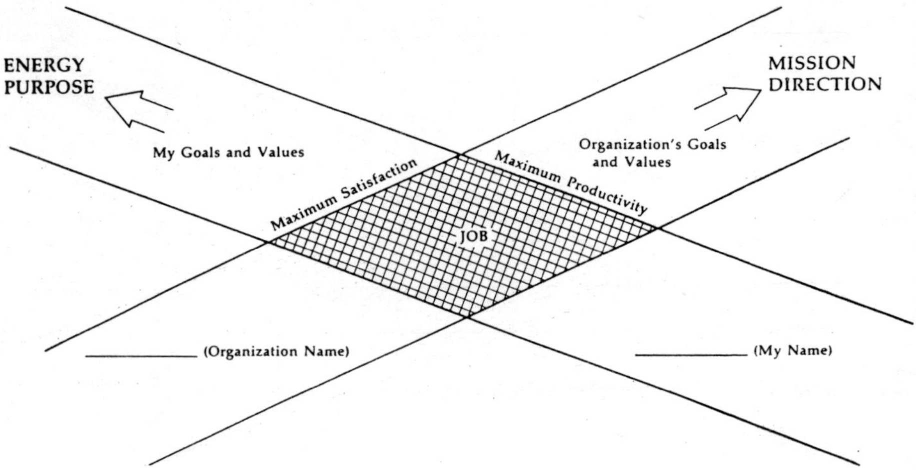

When you tie these two components together—organization direction with personal energy—you will be much closer to maximum satisfaction and productivity than most employees.

Exercise 1: A Goal Self-Assessment

1. The purpose of my organization is:

2. The purpose of my job is:

3. Some of the daily responsibilities in my job are:

4. The three most important priorities of my job are:

1)

2)

3)

If you had difficulty completing the information in Exercise 1, you may find that you and your boss are not in tune. To create an effective partnership with your boss, it is essential to know your boss' most important priorities.

Exercise 2: Questionnaire for Employees*

Please complete this questionnaire on your own. Check those that apply.

About Your Manager

1. Does your manager prefer to receive information through:

____ Memos ____ Phone calls

____ Formal meetings ____ Informal meetings

____ Other (specify) ____________________

2. What is your manager's preferred style of working?

____ Organized and highly structured

____ Moderately organized and structured

____ Little organization or structure

____ Other (specify) ____________________

3. What are your manager's top three organizational priorities?

1. ____________________
2. ____________________
3. ____________________

4. What are your manager's top three personal priorities?

1. ____________________
2. ____________________
3. ____________________

5. What is your manager's attitude toward conflict?

____ Thrives on it ____ Tries to minimize it

____ Other (specify) ____________________

6. What are your manager's three outstanding strengths?

1. ____________________
2. ____________________
3. ____________________

*This questionnaire was designed by Pryor Resources, Inc. It will help you and your supervisor clarify what your job should look like, including top priorities and direction.

7. What is your manager's greatest pressure? ____________________

8. What will your manager say are your three greatest strengths?

   1. ____________________
   2. ____________________
   3. ____________________

9. What will your manager say are your top three organizational priorities?

   1. ____________________
   2. ____________________
   3. ____________________

10. What will your manager say are your top three personal priorities?

   1. ____________________
   2. ____________________
   3. ____________________

About You—Change perspective to focus on your point of view

11. Do you prefer to receive information through:

____ Memos ____ Phone calls

____ Formal meetings ____ Informal meetings

____ Other (specify) ____________________

12. What is your preferred style of working?

____ Organized and highly structured

____ Moderately organized and structured

____ Little organization or structure

____ Other (specify) ____________________

13. What is your greatest pressure? ____________________

14. What is your attitude toward conflict?

____ Thrive on it

____ Try to minimize it

____ Other (specify) ____________________

Exercise 3: Questionnaire for Bosses

Please copy this questionnaire and ask your boss to complete it from the management perspective. Then compare your answers and come to an understanding about your priorities and working styles.

About You—the boss

1. Do you prefer to receive information through:

____ Memos

____ Formal meetings

____ Phone calls

____ Informal meetings

____ Other (specify) ____________________

2. What is your preferred style of working?

____ Organized and highly structured

____ Moderately organized and structured

____ Little organization or structure

____ Other (specify) ____________________

3. What are your top three organizational priorities?

1. ____________________
2. ____________________
3. ____________________

4. What are your top three personal priorities?

1. ____________________
2. ____________________
3. ____________________

5. What is your attitude toward conflict?

____ Thrive on it

____ Try to minimize it

____ Other (specify) ____________________

6. What do you see as your three outstanding strengths?
   1. ____________________
   2. ____________________
   3. ____________________

7. What is your greatest pressure? ____________________

8. What are your employee's three greatest strengths?
   1. ____________________
   2. ____________________
   3. ____________________

9. What are your employee's top three organizational goals?
   1. ____________________
   2. ____________________
   3. ____________________

10. What are your employee's top three personal priorities?
    1. ____________________
    2. ____________________
    3. ____________________

11. Does your employee prefer to receive information through:

    ____ Memos ____ Phone calls

    ____ Formal meetings ____ Informal meetings

    ____ Other (specify) ____________________

12. What is your employee's preferred style of working?

    ____ Organized and highly structured

    ____ Moderately organized and structured

    ____ Little organization or structure

    ____ Other (specify) ____________________

13. What is your employee's greatest pressure? ____________________

14. What is your employee's attitude toward conflict?

    ____ Thrives on it ____ Tries to minimize it

    ____ Other (specify) ____________________

Exercise 4: Check Your Assumptions

If you had difficulty coming up with answers about your supervisor, priorities and organization's goals, discuss the answers with your boss. Here are other strategies that may help. Check the approaches that you want to use.

____ **1.** Ask about goals during a one-to-one meeting with your supervisor. You might say, "I have been trying to improve my performance and it would be helpful to have a clearer picture of how my work goals fit in with yours and the company's." (Make a copy of Exercise 3. Give it to your boss if you have not already done so.)

____ **2.** Encourage discussion during a staff meeting. You could say, "As a member of this working team, I feel it's important for us to agree on common goals. Could we discuss them and write them down?"

____ **3.** Send a written memo: "To make sure I am going in the right direction, I have developed a list of my five key goals for the next six months. Please review them and let me know if I am on target. Correct any areas of misunderstanding."

____ **4.** Encourage your boss and associates to share progress reports regarding collective and individual achievement of goals and objectives. Use team meetings to discuss problems and ways to overcome them by working together more effectively.

Add More

____

____

____

____

____

____

____

____

____

____

OTHER WAYS TO FIND OUT YOUR BOSS' PRIORITIES

Asking questions is not the only way to assess your boss's priorities. Just by being alert, you can pick up valuable information. Be on the lookout for expressions and ideas used most often by your company's management personnel. Here are some ways you can go about collecting these phrases:

- Read messages posted on bulletin boards, company newsletters, memos from your chief executive officer, annual reports and stock market reports. Highlight how your company describes its goals, competition and problems. Try to find repeated key words such as ''innovation,'' ''service to customers,'' ''excellence,'' ''commitment.''

- Listen to themes that arise in meetings. For example, one committee includes this goal on every meeting agenda: ''To involve total membership in decision making.''

- In small businesses, goals may not be stated so publicly. Listen to what gets everyone excited and frustrated. You may hear people talking about ''building repeat business'' and ''making sure that everything is done right the first time.''

BLEND GOALS

Your goals and your supervisor's goals do not need to be identical, but they need to be compatible. Supervisors and employees can start out with opposing goals and change them to complementary goals.

Noncompatible Goals

Boss:	"To improve teamwork in my department."
Employee:	"To work independently on projects I can control totally."

Compatible Goals

Boss:	"To improve teamwork in my department."
Employee:	"To work collaboratively with my associates on project teams and to target a few projects or parts of team projects I can handle independently."

Exercise 5: Compatible Goals

Based upon the discussion with my boss, we agreed that my organizational priorities are:

____

____

____

____

____

____

____

____

BLOCKS TO GOAL ACHIEVEMENT

Even after you and your supervisor agree on professional goals, achieving those goals may require the ability to overcome barriers or "blocks." A block is anything that prevents you from reaching desired outcomes, causing frustration and pressure. Typical blocks include:

- Personal problems such as poor health, anxiety about family, lack of knowledge or skills and low self-esteem
- Stress caused by the organizational environment, including constant criticism, rumors, poor communication, unclear expectations or directions, poor physical working conditions and inadequate supplies
- External pressures such as economic recession, low customer demand and excessive competition

Blocks to Goal Achievement

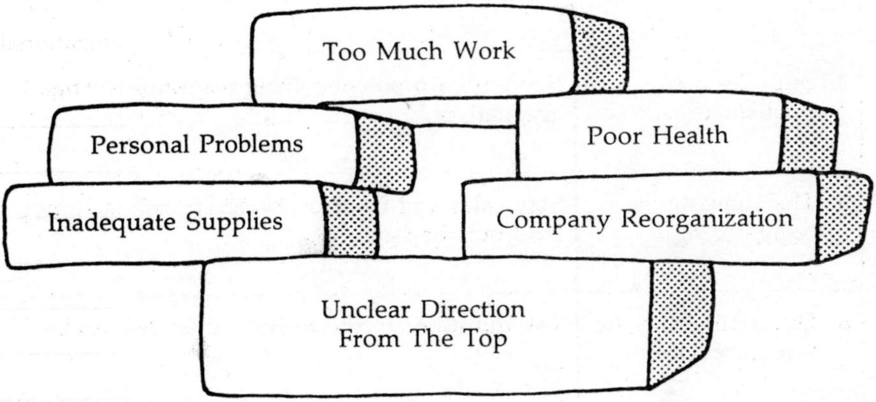

OVERCOMING BLOCKS

One of the most valuable skills an employee can bring to any workplace is the ability to overcome obstacles while remaining flexible and calm. Following is a list of typical blocks to an effective employee-employer partnership, with suggestions for how to become a ''block buster.'' Think about how they apply to you.

Blocks	What I Could Do to Overcome Blocks
1. There is just too much work	Organize work better. Suggest that our department/ team discuss how we can work more cooperatively and reduce unnecessary interruptions. Document work load and suggest hiring permanent or temporary staff.
2. Poor health	Exercise regularly. Eat breakfast every day. Get a checkup. Have specialists study workplace hazards, such as ventilation, lighting, workstation ergonomics, and make recommendations.
3. Boss has family/ personal problems	Be empathetic but avoid in-depth personal discussions.
4. Supplies are inadequate	Serve on a problem-solving team to investigate alternatives.
5. The company is reorganizing	Stay calm and flexible. Avoid spreading rumors. Find out the facts.
6. Directions from the top are unclear	Ask questions, write memos, offer feedback.
7. The economy is in a recession	Suggest ways to reduce costs and waste.

Exercise 6: Create An Action Plan

Now list your own ideas for becoming a block buster.

Blocks	What I Could Do to Overcome Blocks
1.	
2.	
3.	

SECTION

III

Communicate with Impact

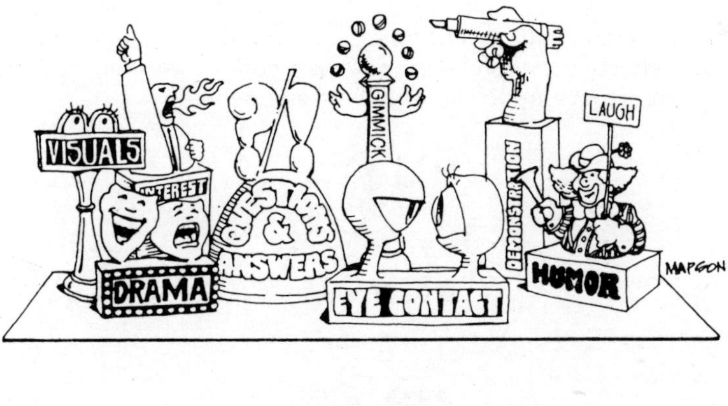

The quality of a partnership between an employee and boss depends on the quality of communication between the two. Communication does not imply that supervisors and staff will agree with each other, but at its best, communication means they will understand each other.

WHAT IS EFFECTIVE COMMUNICATION?

Sometimes our own feelings of powerlessness or inferiority may interfere with communicating effectively with a boss. These feelings of inferiority can come from past professional experiences, our own parent–child relationship, or the negative things we say to ourselves (''My boss knows a lot more about this than I do—I'm sure my point of view isn't needed.'') Although you need to have a healthy respect for your manager, it is also important to view your own talents and contributions as worthwhile and important.

If you recognize that it is difficult to talk with your supervisor, plan on ways to counteract those negative emotions. It is particularly important with new bosses to come to the relationship without preconceived notions about what they may be or should be like.

Before meeting with your manager, practice saying positive things to yourself or a co-worker, such as, ''I have a lot of experience with this organization and my analytical skills are excellent. I know you will want my input on project xyz . . .'' Write an outline of what you want to cover. The more you can plan the conversation, the more effective your interaction with your boss will be.

The two primary ingredients of effective communication are effective expression and effective comprehension. When both of these ingredients are present, you can achieve understanding between people.

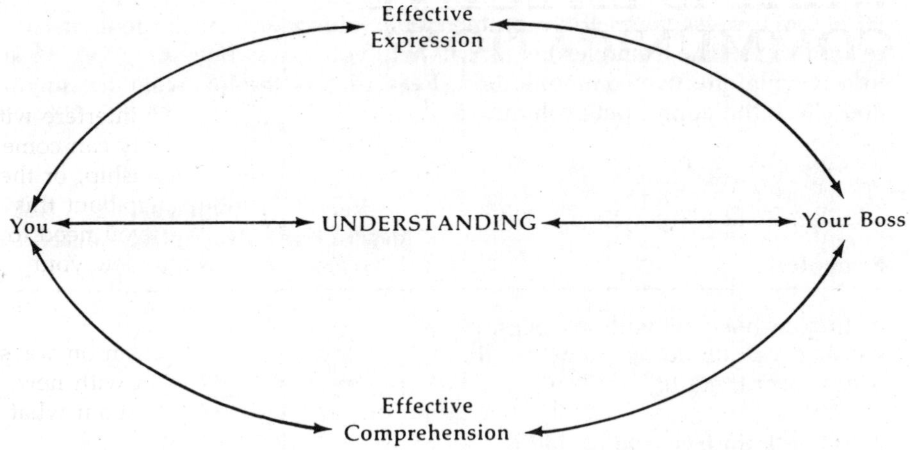

When effective expression or effective comprehension are not present, instead of *understanding,* you will experience a *communication gap.*

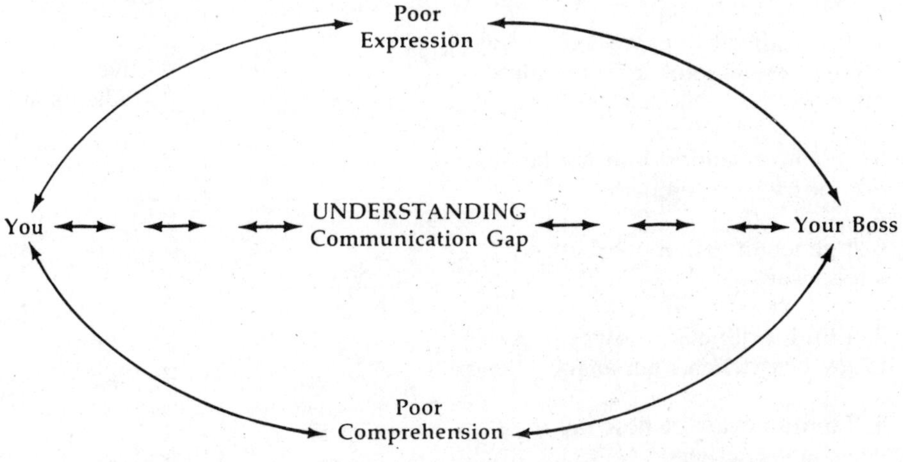

"The spoken word belongs half to him who speaks, and half to him who hears."

A French Proverb

Exercise 1: How Well Do You Express Yourself?

How you express yourself has an incredible impact on your professional relationships. The examples below will help you assess how effective you are in achieving effective communication. Read each of the following statements and check the appropriate column.

Examples	Very descriptive of me	Somewhat descriptive of me	Not descriptive of me
1. In conversations with my boss, my words generally do not come out the way I want them to.	________	________	________
2. When I am trying to explain something, others have a tendency to put words in my mouth.	________	________	________
3. I usually assume my boss knows what I am trying to say without my explaining it.	________	________	________
4. It is difficult to express my ideas if they are different from the ideas of my boss.	________	________	________
5. In conversations with my boss, I do not try to be empathetic.	________	________	________
6. I generally talk more than my supervisor.	________	________	________
7. I find it difficult to express myself to my boss when I am angry.	________	________	________
8. I am unaware of how my tone of voice affects others.	________	________	________
9. I sometimes say things that hurt others or create conflict.	________	________	________

Examples	Very descriptive of me	Somewhat descriptive of me	Not descriptive of me
10. I do not disagree with my boss because I am afraid s/he will get angry.	________	________	________
11. I find it uncomfortable to compliment others.	________	________	________
12. When a problem arises between me and my manager, I cannot discuss it without becoming angry.	________	________	________
13. I do not try to use words that my manager will understand.	________	________	________
14. I ramble when I try to explain something.	________	________	________

Discussion

Review the answers in the "Very descriptive of me" column. These are the areas that probably hinder your manager's comprehension of what you say. Think about your relationship with your boss. Jot down the communication areas in which you need to improve and examples of how those problem areas have affected your relationship to date.

1. Problem Area: ____

Result: ____

2. Problem Area: ____

Result: ____

3. Problem Area: ____

Result: ____

COMMUNICATION GAPS

Before you can devise strategies for improving the way you express yourself, you need to understand the causes of ineffective communication. Some of the gaps in your communication may occur for the following reasons:

1. **Vocabulary Failure.** Words are tools for thought and expression. If you do not know the exact meaning of words, you cannot think with precision; therefore, your ability to express ideas and feelings is also diminished. Studies indicate that people with the highest vocabularies are also highest in position and pay.

   Action Ideas: Read everything you can get your hands on. Listen to Nightingale-Conant's tape series, *The Verbal Advantage.* Get a word-a-day calendar for your desk.

2. **Talking Too Much.** Some of us judge others' acceptance of us by how much we talk and how much others listen to us. But you can overwhelm your listeners with conversation until they become confused, bored or both.

   Action Ideas: Learn to be word-effective. Do not waste words or ramble. Get to the point, keep to the point. Become aware of how much you dominate conversations and why. Do you begin talking more when you are nervous or uncomfortable? Try to pick up on your listener's interest level.

3. Speaking Before Thinking. Sometimes we speak before thinking. You may not think through why you want to speak; you may not be taking time to assess the best way to express your ideas.

Action Ideas: Stop before you jump into a conversation and ask yourself: What do I want to say? Why do I want to say this? What is the best way for me to get the message across? In a formal setting, you may want to outline your ideas before expressing yourself. For very difficult conversations, it is helpful to practice your comments in advance.

4. Not Testing For Understanding. The speaker may fail to make sure that the listener understands what has been communicated. Testing for understanding minimizes the possibility of a communication gap and avoids misunderstandings.

Action Ideas: Ask questions to see if your listener has understood your message. Women generally ask more questions in a conversation than men. They do this several ways, such as ending a statement on a higher pitch, or using tag-ons such as ''O K?'' ''All right?'' or ''Do you agree?''

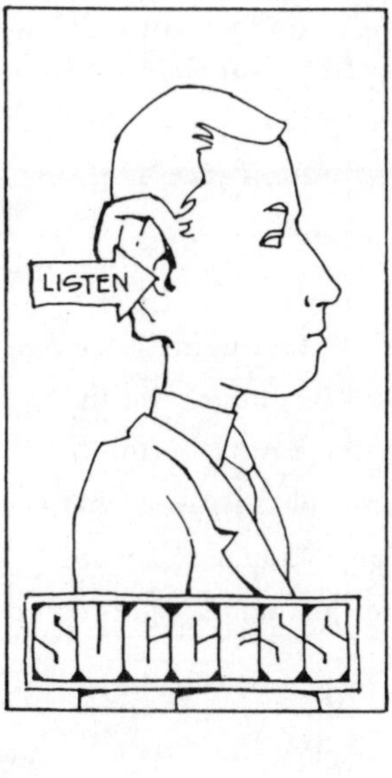

Exercise 2: My Communication Gaps

Listed below are some of the communication gaps that cause problems in the way I express myself:

1. Gap: ______________________________

   Action Idea: ______________________________

2. Gap: ______________________________

   Action Idea: ______________________________

3. Gap: ______________________________

   Action Idea: ______________________________

How Well Do You Comprehend or Listen?

Since communication is a two-way process, it is as important to analyze how well you comprehend or listen to others as it is to know how well you express yourself. We spend more than half our day listening, yet we retain very little of what we hear. One study concluded that we hear half of what is said, listen to half of what we hear, understand half of that, believe half of that, and remember only half of that. Translated into an eight-hour day, it means:

We spend about four hours listening.

We hear about two hour's worth.

We listen to one hour's worth.

We understand 30 minutes of that hour.

We believe only 15 minute's worth.

We remember just under eight minute's worth.

Exercise 3: Self-Assessment in Listening

Assess your comprehension and listening skills by evaluating how often you engage in these poor listening habits when listening to your boss:

Problem Area	Almost Always 1	2	3	4	Almost Never 5
1. Disinterested in subject matter because it does not affect my job	1	2	3	4	5
2. Overly critical when manager speaks	1	2	3	4	5
3. Interrupt	1	2	3	4	5
4. Focus on details and miss main points	1	2	3	4	5
5. Fake attention because it is "the same old story."	1	2	3	4	5
6. Avoid difficult topics	1	2	3	4	5
7. Allow distractions to interfere	1	2	3	4	5
8. Daydream in staff meetings	1	2	3	4	5
9. Allow emotional reactions to certain words or my boss to block the message	1	2	3	4	5
10. Give negative nonverbal cues	1	2	3	4	5

TOTAL ______ (out of a possible 50)

Scoring:

50–35: You are an excellent listener!
34–29: You are doing a good job.
28–23: You could use some improvement.
Below 23: Keep reading!

COMMUNICATION GAPS (continued)

► **CAPITALIZE ON THOUGHT SPEED**

Most people speak at a rate of 125 words per minute, yet can listen at about 500 words per minute. Because of this, you might find that you sometimes daydream, interrupt your boss or fake your attention. What you do with your "extra" thinking time can spell the difference between being an effective or poor listener.

► **JUDGE CONTENT, NOT DELIVERY**

Many listeners focus only on a speaker's appearance or personality. Force yourself to concentrate on the message being communicated and how the information can help you.

► **RESIST DISTRACTIONS**

A good listener fights distractions. Sometimes distractions can be easily handled by closing a door, turning off the radio or asking your supervisor to talk louder. If you cannot eliminate the distraction, you may simply need to concentrate more. Take notes; this sends the message that your supervisor's ideas are important.

► **HOLD YOUR FIRE**

If you are upset by something your boss said, the tendency is to ignore the rest of the message and concentrate on your rebuttal. Sometimes, by listening to the remainder of your supervisor's message, your need for rebuttal will be eliminated. Do not interrupt or make assumptions about your manager's message.

► **HEAR WHAT IS SAID**

People often fail to understand what is said, even if they hear it directly, because they hear only what they want to hear. They employ selective listening.

You may listen more selectively to a problem boss to validate your dislike and their lack of competence. By hearing and retaining only what you want to hear, you may be filtering out critical information.

► **WORK AT LISTENING**

Listening is hard work and most of us have never been formally trained how to do it. To be a good listener, you must be an active participant. Keep in mind that if you rearrange the letters in the word "listen," you get "silent." You cannot listen when you are talking.

Exercise 4: Personal Action Plan for Better Communication

I have problems listening or comprehending what my manager says for the following reasons:

____

____

____

These are the ways I plan to increase my listening and comprehension effectiveness:

____

____

____

____

____

____

Understanding takes two things:
talking and listening.
When we talk, we open the way for others
into our private thoughts and feelings,
and when we listen,
we step through the door
into another person's point of view.
Talking and listening—
with them come understanding.
And with understanding can come
some of life's most important things—
respect and acceptance and love.

Unknown

SECTION IV

Talk's Not Cheap: Building Bridges via Meetings

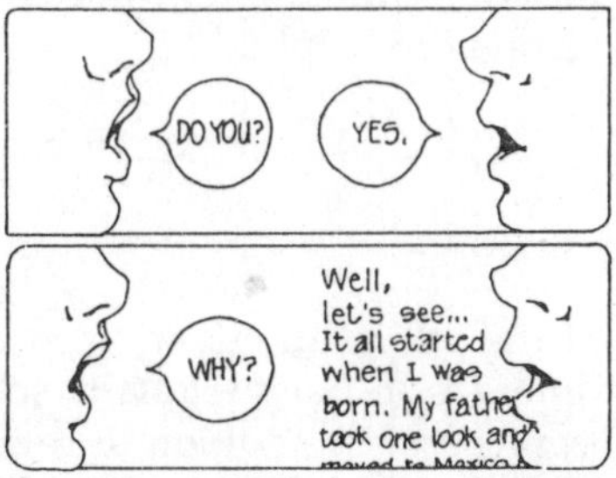

The basic ingredients needed for effective communication are expression, comprehension and listening. You can use those concepts to build a more effective partnership with your boss. Meetings are effective methods to build bridges of understanding.

We communicate for four basic reasons:

1. To build relationships
2. To express feelings
3. To exchange information so we can do our jobs, achieve goals and learn
4. To persuade, inspire and motivate others

Exercise 1: Why We Communicate

Think about the times you have communicated with your boss and your role in each of those situations. Then answer the following questions:

Which was more important—to be a good expressor of information or comprehender/listener of information, or both? Why?

____

____

____

____

In which situations is it difficult to communicate effectively with your boss?

____

____

____

____

We need different skills to communicate different needs. Knowing which skills to use and when to use them is helpful.

Let's Talk!

One of the best ways to elicit the information you need to do your job and increase your team's effectiveness is to have regularly scheduled private meetings between you and your boss, in addition to regularly scheduled staff meetings. These meetings can improve communication between you and your boss, resolve problems and increase partnership accountability.

In a study conducted by R. Wayne Boss, professor at the University of Colorado Graduate School of Business Administration, regular manager-employee meetings had a positive effect on organization climate, team effectiveness and productivity. Participants in the study cited not just increased quantity of time with their supervisor, but improved quality of supervisor-employee communication. Naturally, the trust level between supervisor and employees also improved, because regularly addressing conflict prevented problems from growing.

BEFORE YOU JUMP IN . . .

Before you suggest a bi-weekly or weekly meeting with your manager, prepare a list of reasons and benefits for having this meeting. You may have to sell your supervisor on this idea. The reasons and benefits Wayne Boss discovered in his study may fit your particular partnership. Check those that apply to your situation:

Reasons For Bi-Weekly Meetings:

____ To discuss administrative or organizational problems and suggestions for resolutions

____ To resolve any interpersonal problems between you and your boss before they create more difficulties

____ To discuss personal problems faced by either person that may impede your job

____ To identify individual or organizational issues

____ To provide an opportunity for mini-training sessions in administrative, technical and management skills. To prepare you for promotion opportunities or temporary supervisory responsibilities (in your manager's absence)

____ To share information about what is happening in the organization

____ To set short- and long-term goals

____ To review action items from previous meetings

Benefits of Bi-weekly Meetings:

____ Positive effect on team morale

____ Will hold everyone accountable; therefore, timely completion of assignments will increase

____ Improved quantity and quality of boss-employee communication

____ Time savings and fewer interruptions

____ Improved trust between boss and employee

____ Quality of weekly staff meetings improves because meetings now concentrate on matters involving the entire staff versus individual staff members

____ Fewer problems because conflicts are addressed regularly, preventing problems from growing

GETTING STARTED

To have an effective meeting, prepare and use an agenda. Without it, the meeting can turn into a gripe session or social hour. Eventually, both you and your supervisor should create an agenda together. Initially, until your boss realizes the benefits of the meeting, you may have to develop the agenda.

Meetings can be short, but they must be held regularly. To use the time most effectively, limit the discussion for each agenda item and allow no interruptions. You may want to hold your meeting in a conference room without a phone, or in your office where you can make arrangements to have the phone calls forwarded. Time is wasted when meetings are interrupted, because it takes twice as long to overcome the interruption than it takes to endure it.

When an organization is in crisis, meetings should be more frequent and brief. For example, hospital staffs would benefit from two short daily meetings, rather than one long meeting, so they can cope with the minute-to-minute crises in their environment.

Below is a sample bi-weekly meeting outline used by a sales manager with her boss.

Sample Bi-Weekly Meeting Outline:

1. **"Good news" reports.** Both employee and boss have one minute to share some good news about the past two weeks. It can be either business-related or personal. Good news reports get the meeting off to a positive start and get both parties involved. *Example:* "Both sales reps met their quota for the second week in a row."

2. **Business update.** Update each other on profits, losses, upcoming sales incentive programs, etc. Discuss business or competition news. This is where most other agenda items would fall.

3. **Problem solving.** Discuss administrative or organizational problems and suggestions for resolutions. Discuss any interpersonal or individual problems that are getting in the way.

4. **Bi-weekly priorities.** Each person should go over his or her two-week goals and any special projects he or she is working on. Realign priorities and set short- and long-term goals.

5. **Next meeting's agenda items.** Ask what the boss would like to discuss at your next meeting and create the new agenda.

SAMPLE AGENDA

Bi-Weekly Meeting — (Date)		Time
1. Good News Reports	both	2 min.
2. Business Update		
—Review action plan from previous meeting	Carla	10 min.
—Upcoming exhibits	Chris	5 min.
—Sales report	Carla	10 min.
—Procedure x overview	Chris	15 min.
3. Problem solving		
—Sales reps' tickler system	Carla	10 min.
—Missing call-backs	Chris	5 min.
4. Two Week Priorities	both	10 min.
5. Action Plan	Carla	5 min.
6. Next Meeting's Agenda	both	3 min.

GETTING ACTION FROM BI-WEEKLY MEETINGS

To make your bi-weekly meetings effective, you may need to follow them up with a memo. Many companies have found the Meeting Action Plan useful. You may want to try it, too.

MEETING ACTION PLAN

Meeting Date/Time: ____________________

Leader: ____________ Recorder: ____________

Action to be Taken	Person Responsible	Deadline Completed

Time Meeting Started: ________ Ended: ________ Length: ________

Next Meeting Scheduled (Date): ____________________

Time Begin: ____________ End: ____________

THE HIGH COST OF MEETINGS

This simple formula can help you figure out how much one of your regular meetings costs your organization.

Exercise 3: The High Cost of Meetings

1. List a weekly/monthly meeting ______________________

2. Time preparing for meeting ______

3. Time attending the meeting + ______

Subtotal ______

4. Number of attendees ______

5. Multiply #3 (subtotal) × #4 = ______

6. Multiply #4 × average hourly wage $ = ______

Average Cost for Meeting $ ______

Exercise 4: Examining the Effectiveness of Meetings

Assess the meetings that you attend regularly. Consider costs as well as problems that need attention.

1. List the regular meetings that you attend. How would you rate their effectiveness on a scale of 1 to 5 (1 = very ineffective, a total waste of my time, to 5 = very effective):

Meeting **Rating**

____

____

2. What are the major problems with the meetings you attend?

____

____

3. What have you done to increase the effectiveness of those meetings?

____

____

IF YOUR BOSS IS THE MEETING LEADER

If your boss is the meeting leader and you cannot avoid the meeting, you may be able to forestall some difficulties. Here are some suggestions.

1. **Problem:** No agenda

Solutions: Suggest privately to your manager that agendas can speed up meetings and increase their productivity and effectiveness. Provide a sample agenda and, if needed, assist in developing this one.

Volunteer to take notes on the Action Plan. Once the group is committed to the idea and can see the benefits, rotate that responsibility.

Volunteer to explain the benefits and purpose of the agenda at the first meeting where it is implemented.

2. **Problem:** Meetings consistently go over scheduled time frame

Solutions: Suggest scheduling the meeting right before lunch, before another engagement or before quitting time. Most people will not allow a meeting to run into their personal time.

Ask that time frames be assigned to each agenda item. Volunteer to be the official time keeper so that no one goes over their time. Rotate this responsibility once the group can see and appreciate the benefits of doing so.

3. **Problem:** Speakers ramble

Solutions: When the speaker stops for a breath, rephrase one of the statements and make a comment to get back on track. Ask for someone else's opinion. Ask your boss if the group can move on to the next agenda item.

Refer to the agenda, and ask which topic the speaker is discussing. Say, "I'm sorry, but I guess I'm a little lost. How is this related to the topic?"

4. Problem: Interruptions

Solutions: Discuss privately with the meeting leader how attendance can be limited to only those people most appropriate and explain the benefits of keeping the participants to a minimum.

Volunteer to facilitate the meeting. Tell the group you will start the meeting on time and then do it.

Suggest holding a ''stand up'' meeting, if appropriate.

Discuss the interruption problem during the meeting. As a group, define what constitutes an emergency and when the group should allow interruptions. Put a message board outside the meeting room so the group can check for messages at breaks. Get the group to commit to allowing no interruptions. One organization scheduled 15-minute breaks every hour to accommodate their specific environment.

Exercise 5: Meeting Action Ideas

Create your own action plan for more efficient meetings. Return to Exercise 3 and jot down major problems with the meetings you attend:

____

____

____

What will you do to increase the effectiveness of those meetings?

____

____

____

____

____

____

S E C T I O N

V

Confronting with Compassion

Criticizing anyone, especially your supervisor, is difficult and requires sensitivity. However, if you can learn this art, your work life may improve. Criticism can uncover problems early, which can lead to early solutions and save time. If correctly handled, criticism encourages both the critic and the one criticized—even bosses—to learn and grow.

HOW CAN YOU CRITIQUE YOUR MANAGER?

Examine your attitude toward giving criticism and some of the pitfalls you may encounter.

Exercise 1: Criticism Pitfalls

Check the attitudes you have that inhibit your giving criticism:

____ If I wait long enough, the situation will probably resolve itself, so I do not have to get involved

____ Since I do not like to receive criticism, I cannot imagine my supervisor would; therefore, I choose to ignore the problem

____ I criticize indirectly by using sarcasm or jokes

____ I would rather complain to my co-workers than criticize my manager directly

____ There never seems to be a right time to criticize, and I keep putting off giving criticism

____ It takes so much time to criticize effectively, I would rather do more work than take the time to give feedback to my supervisor

____ I am unsure of how my manager will respond to my criticism; therefore, I avoid giving it

____ I am not perfect, and my boss has so much more experience than I do; who am I to judge my supervisor's behavior?

____ If I give my boss negative feedback, it may be used against me at my next performance evaluation

____ I have let the situation go on for too long now, and I am so angry that I am sure I'm going to blow up and mishandle the situation

The more of these attitudes you checked, the more difficulty you will have criticizing anyone, particularly your boss.

For an excellent resource on criticism, read *Giving and Receiving Criticism* by Patti Hathaway, also published by Crisp Publications, Inc.

CRITICIZING YOUR BOSS

One study found that people without supervisory responsibilities found it more difficult to criticize than those who have supervisory responsibilities. More people (51%) find it difficult to criticize their boss, and regardless of whom they criticize, it is most difficult getting started.

Some people ignore problematic situations and hope that if they wait long enough the situation will disappear. Avoiding the situation may be appropriate when the issue is trivial or if the problem is symptomatic of more pressing problems. However, ignoring a situation is inappropriate most of the time because most problems do not go away on their own; they usually escalate.

Some people refuse to criticize, for fear their boss will not like them or may give them a negative performance review. Criticizing your boss may result in conflict, but avoiding conflict at all costs will not solve the problem either.

Because many people are uncomfortable receiving feedback, we are reluctant to give it. This contradicts most research conducted on motivation, which suggests that feedback is one of the biggest motivators for change. Even bosses can appreciate well thought-out feedback and criticism.

Providing negative feedback or criticism to your boss can be very delicate. People have been known to cheat, lie and kill to save face. Neither forget nor underestimate your boss' need to preserve his/her reputation and dignity.

Exercise 2: Criticism Analysis

Before you criticize your boss, figure out the specifics of your criticism, as well as your motives. Complete the following analysis:

1. Describe the situation and problem you are experiencing with your boss.

____

____

____

2. When did this problem start, and what is the impact on you?

____

____

____

3. How do you think your boss will react to your criticism? What are the risks involved in providing this feedback?

____

____

____

4. What are the benefits to you if this problem is resolved?

____

____

____

5. Do the benefits far outweigh the costs? Yes / No / Not Sure (Explain)

____

____

____

If you answered "no" to the last question, the costs are too high. You will probably not want to criticize your supervisor. You might want to think through other options for coping with this situation. If your answer is "yes" or you are not sure, the five S's of providing unsolicited feedback will help you criticize your boss:

FIVE S's OF PROVIDING UNSOLICITED FEEDBACK

STEP 1: SELECT YOUR TIMING

Timing is critical. If your boss is under considerable stress, wait for a better time. Pick the time and place carefully to avoid interruptions or distractions. Set an appointment rather than dropping in so that your boss senses the importance of the discussion.

STEP 2: SECURE THE BOSS' PERMISSION

Tell your supervisor you have something that will help both of you to become more effective. Don't negate the information by saying, "It's really not that big of a deal, but . . ." Say, "I think I have some information that would be helpful to our team. Could we schedule a time so that we could discuss my ideas?"

Do not skip over your boss and take your problems to your boss' supervisor. Bypassing your manager leaves you with little credibility, even if your points are valid ones. Also, do not criticize your supervisor publicly or to your co-workers; it is unprofessional and unacceptable behavior.

STEP 3: SHARE SPECIFICS

Get your facts straight. If you cannot provide specific examples of the problems you are discussing, your boss will most likely dismiss your comments. An effective formula for giving criticism to your manager is the DASS script described on the next page.

THE DASS SCRIPT

This is how a DASS Script works:

DESCRIBE: (the exact behavior you find bothersome) "When you . . ."

ACKNOWLEDGE: (what you really feel about the manager's behavior or situation) "I feel . . ."

SPECIFY: (ask for a different, specified behavior) "What I would prefer . . ."

SHOW TEAM BENEFITS: (what is in it for the manager and the team) "This is how you will benefit . . ."

DASS Script Examples

Poor Version	Better Version
DESCRIBE "You never start and end staff meetings on time."	"When we end staff meetings late, I am late for my next appointment."
ACKNOWLEDGE "You make me so angry I could scream."	"I feel frustrated and rushed the rest of the day."
SPECIFY "Why don't you learn how to manage?"	"What I would prefer is that we would set a realistic ending time on our staff meetings."
SHOW TEAM BENEFITS	"That way we could all make better use of our time after the meeting and increase our productivity and time effectiveness."

We often omit the action-oriented *specify* step. A part of us really wants an apology from the other person after we tell him or her how we feel. One of the most important steps in criticizing people is specifying actions they can take. Then the other person can do something about the criticism, rather than defensively react to our disclosure of negative feelings. Offer to help if you can.

STEP 4: SHOW TEAM BENEFITS

Show your boss the benefits that will accrue to the entire work team by a change of behavior. You want to build up, not pull down, your boss.

STEP 5: SUMMARIZE YOUR AGREEMENT

Summarize what has been discussed and confirm your mutual commitment. Show enthusiasm for the plans made. Be positive. Show your willingness and interest in improving yourself. Each time you work with your boss or are completing a project, ask, "How could I have improved my performance?" Give your boss an opportunity to make other suggestions. Close the discussion on a friendly, upbeat note. "I really appreciate your willingness to discuss this and I am confident our team is going to benefit from these changes. Thank you."

Exercise 3: Providing Unsolicited Feedback to Your Boss

Complete the following action plan on giving unsolicited criticism to your boss. Choose a specific criticism you wish to give.

Step 1: Select your timing. When is the best time to criticize your boss?

____

____

____

Step 2: Secure their permission. How are you going to gain their permission?

____

____

____

Step 3: Share specifics. Using the *DASS* script, jot down your thoughts.

Describe (the behavior you find bothersome):

"When you . . . ______________________________"

Acknowledge (what you feel):

"I feel . . . ______________________________"

Specify (ask for a different, specified behavior):

"What I would prefer . . . ______________________________"

Show team benefits:

"I really appreciate your interest and know that this will positively affect our team by . . . ______________________________

Thanks!"

S E C T I O N

VI

How to Read Your Boss

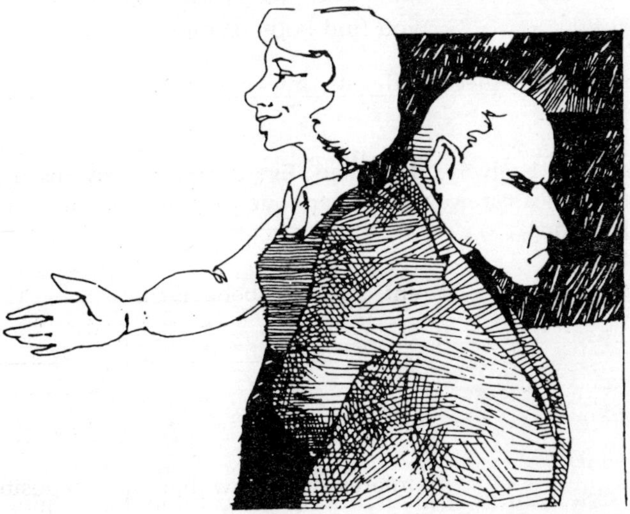

Even the best efforts of competent employees are stymied if they do not have information about their particular boss' needs, preferences, motivators and demotivators. As a result, supervisors may perceive that their staff is resistant, incapable, disloyal, uncooperative or even incompetent. Employees may perceive that their supervisor is unpredictable, unclear or uncaring.

Exercise 1: Complaints and Frustrations

Following is a list of common complaints expressed by people who do not understand their managers. Check the statements that characterize your frustrations with your supervisor.

____ My boss thrives on chaos that s/he creates.

____ I never complete an assignment because of all the last minute revisions and rewrites.

____ My boss talks so much during staff meetings that we never get out on time and we adjourn with the agenda only partially completed.

____ My manager is so specific about how I should do my work that there really is no room for my creativity.

____ My supervisor is so cautious about making changes that it is impossible to get a timely decision.

____ Our team starts a project and then our manager gives us five more things to do.

____ By rushing and neglecting details, my boss creates crises that I have to resolve.

____ My supervisor is always distracted. Even while we are discussing a project, he takes care of other telephone calls and people who stop by to ask questions.

____ Other (specify) ____

____

____

Many working styles can be accommodated in a comfortable relationship, but balance and initiative are necessary. If the employee respects an employer's need for speedy communication, in all likelihood the employer will reciprocate by respecting the employee's need for more information. Usually the employee must act first.

READING YOUR BOSS

Everyone has predictable behavioral patterns. As you learn why people behave in certain ways, you will learn to communicate better. The READ method* can increase your boss-observation skills. The steps are:

R = **Review the signs**

E = **Evaluate established patterns**

A = **Apply appropriate approach**

D = **Do something daily**

STEP 1: R = Review

Working with your boss every day is like driving to work every day. After taking the same route many times, the driver does not pay much attention to the road. So it is with employer and worker. They may endlessly repeat the same practices and wonder why nothing ever improves or changes.

* The READ terminology is derived from the *Personal Profile System,* published by Carlson Learning Company.

Exercise 2: The *STOP* Sign

Pause to read the stop signs along the way. They could signal danger or provide alternate directions. Check at least three behaviors that describe your boss' actions.

Typical Behaviors	Your Boss
1. Carefully plans everything with lists, short- and long-range plans, timelines	P____
2. Seeks perfection in everything; researches every decision	P____
3. Performs routine work and follows schedules such as starting and ending work at the same time every day	S____
4. Experiments with new ideas and projects; takes risks with proven projects	T____
5. Tells people what to do more than asking or convincing them	T____
6. Is very outgoing and friendly, smiles a lot, knows about everyone at work	O____
7. Is very low key; can be depended on to get work done	S____
8. Focuses on end result or goals rather than processes used to get there	T____
9. Asks questions like, "How do people work together? Do they enjoy their work?"	O____
10. Often gives detailed directions on how to do a new assignment	S____
11. Asks, "What is the bottom line, end result or the big picture?"	T____
12. Inquires when evaluating an assignment, "Where is the research on this? How can I be sure it will work?"	P____

Typical Behaviors	Your Boss
13. When stressed, becomes disorganized and talks a lot	**O** ____
14. Office and desk are very neatly organized; has an efficient filing system	**S** ____
15. When communicating with people, is encouraging, supportive, asks their opinions, lets others handle details	**O** ____
16. Communicates precisely based on facts, logic, proven ideas rather than feelings and assumptions	**P** ____

Now count how many of each letter you checked and write it below.

Number Checked

S ____

T ____

O ____

P ____

The highest numbers represent behavior patterns that your supervisor uses most of the time. Stop to think about them. Once you understand these patterns, you can adjust your behavior to improve communications.

STEP 2: E = Evaluate Established Patterns

On the left is a description of each of four behavior patterns represented by the stop sign. On the right is the matching approach most likely to be successful with that behavior.

*** S T O P ***

	Overall Description	Approach
	Supervisors with these behaviors are most likely to:	**The best way to work effectively with this boss is to:**
STEADY	Avoid surprises. Work/communicate well in a small group. Work steadily on routine tasks. Stay neat and organized. Need detailed directions. Have difficulty in an unclear, changing situation.	Be patient. Ask questions and listen. Be quiet and nonconfrontational. Give time to adjust and respond. Emphasize approaches that will minimize risk. Plan action steps. Stay organized yourself. Do not make sudden or drastic changes. Be dependable. Give specific details. Work as part of the team.
TREND SETTER	Act with self confidence. Prefer variety and challenges to a routine job. Be very willing to experiment and set new trends. Take risks and assume leadership roles. Be competitive and controlling. Create chaos with new ventures.	Communicate briefly and directly. If they move recklessly, show how you can help them reach goals faster and better. Be positive. Focus on results, limit details to essentials. Be willing to experiment. Value their innovation. Do not slow them down too much or tell them what to do.

*** S T O P ***

	Overall Description	Approach
OUTGOING	Communicate easily with many people. Prefer flexibility, little control by others. Respond well to recognition and value helping people. Lose focus and waste time with too much talking.	Be friendly, enthusiastic. Listen. Provide opportunities to help people. Organize details, paperwork, scheduling. Be flexible. Value their understanding of people. Include them in discussions, commitees, high-profile projects.
PERFECTIONIST	Want everything to be done right, in compliance with laws, standards, policies and procedures. Dislike chaos or unpredictable working environment. Expect themselves and others to be experts. Become overly critical and demanding of themselves and others.	Provide lots of data patiently. Research facts first, especially if idea departs from established practice. Use strategic planning and statistical information. Value their expertise. Help them make timely decisions. Do outstanding work. Be diplomatic and logical.

STEP 3: A = Apply Appropriate Approach

Now we will take each of the four behavioral patterns and demonstrate how to apply the STOP, READ and DASS guidelines (see Section V for DASS Script).

S

Steadies sometimes have difficulty coping with unusual situations. They prefer to follow established patterns and make changes gradually.

Appropriate approach: Find out what kind of information your boss needs, and identify timelines. Use a friendly, unrushed manner and tone of voice. Suggest ways to minimize risks.

Say, "When my recommendations for improving my department are delayed, it means everyone will have to rush at the last minute. I would prefer to make more timely changes. I would like to discuss a gradual change in the following procedures ________. I have assessed the possible problems and have come up with solutions. What other information would you need to help make a decision? Have I left out anything that you might see as a potential problem if we make this change? I'd like to have a response within a month so we avoid the next crisis."

T

Trend setters are willing to experiment, they like variety, and they like to take risks. Sometimes they create so much change that employees feel they are working in a chaotic environment.

Appropriate approach: Focus on results and ask for priorities. Offer to help make the new ventures successful. A possible script: "When expectations change constantly, it is hard for me to keep up. I feel overwhelmed. What I would prefer is to develop an overall plan and timelines. I would be happy to help in any way possible, such as keeping track of timelines and coordinating our team. We could get others to help out and we would not be in crisis all the time."

O

Outgoing people enjoy conversations and lose track of time easily. They are committed to the democratic process and want people to feel involved and appreciated.

Appropriate approach: ''I enjoy the chance to talk during staff meetings. You really have a talent for bringing people out. However, I feel frustrated that we can't get to the entire agenda. We run late and then I'm late for my next appointments. Maybe we could socialize about 15 minutes at the beginning and again at the end. I could help as time keeper for the agenda. Then we would cover everything and could plan our day better.''

P

Perfectionists always find a better way to do something, and they have trouble knowing when to stop. They have high expectations for themselves and others.

Appropriate approach: Ask more questions in advance and be sure to agree on outcomes, action steps and a timeline. Clarify how much detail and data are required in advance. Several midpoint progress checks would be helpful. Say, ''When I have to rewrite reports, it is difficult to keep up with the deadlines. I feel confused about my role, and I'm not sure if the quality of my work is satisfactory. I'd prefer if we could clarify expectations in advance. I could develop an outline for your review. Then, we could review the report at agreed-upon checkpoints. If we work like this, it would reduce rewrites and wasted time.''

SECTION

VII

The Care and Feeding of a Boss

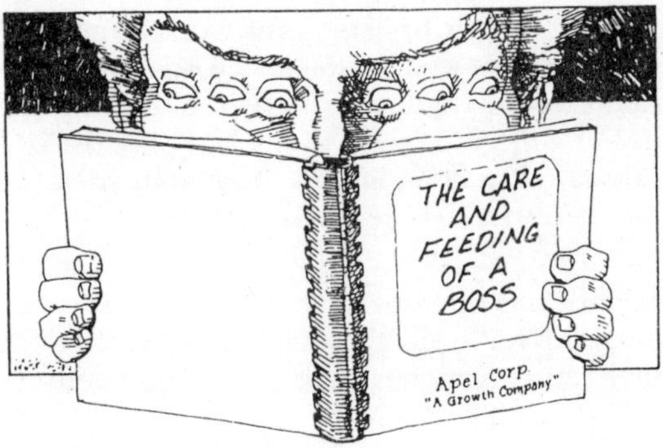

Bosses value many qualities in their employees. In addition to shared professional goals, managers want to see evidence of personal initiative and good thinking skills. Managers from organizations such as banking, manufacturing, education, social service agencies and museums say the following abilities are important to them.

- Decision-making
- Responsibility
- Communication
- Creativity
- Quality
- Time management

SIX WAYS TO BECOME A STAR

You can become a "star employee" by exhibiting the above qualities. Make a commitment to gain these qualities by completing the following exercise. Check each of the following abilities that you intend to improve on in the next six months:

☐ **1. Decision-making**

Although I may occasionally err, I will take a risk rather than do nothing. I will not sit around waiting for someone to tell me what to do. If I see a job that needs to be done, I will do it.

☐ **2. Responsibility**

I will be where I am supposed to be and take responsibility for my actions. I will be willing to work hard, even if it involves overtime. I will get my job done without constant checking and nagging, follow through on my own and tie up loose ends.

☐ **3. Communication**

I will be patient, willing to listen and work at getting along with customers, co-workers and managers. If the boss does something helpful, I will say so. I will provide verbal affirmation without being manipulative. I will go directly to my boss for discussion about problems, rather than complain to other staff members.

☐ **4. Creativity**

I will be flexible and open to change. I will study problems from a different perspective. I will channel my innovative ideas to produce improvement rather than chaos or policy violations.

☐ **5. Quality**

I will deliver services and products with distinction to external and internal customers. I will complete my work so co-workers can do theirs right. I will use my knowledge and job skills with personal pride. I will be willing to improve my own knowledge and skills, understand the company "big picture" and help create it.

☐ **6. Time Management**

I will control unnecessary interruptions in my own work and in interactions with others. I will not waste my boss' time. I will be on time to meetings and lunch. I will meet project deadlines and return telephone calls promptly.

SUCCESSFUL EMPLOYEE ACTIONS

Different companies rank star qualities differently, depending on company culture, personal preferences, the nature of the work and the employee's skill and knowledge. However, some general practices will put you ahead anywhere.

KEEP YOUR BOSS INFORMED

Keeping your boss informed demonstrates at least two of the six abilities: responsibility and communications. Managers from many organizational levels consistently list several areas where they want to be kept informed:

1. **Progress on Projects.**

   Be accountable to your boss on all assigned projects by following through without being reminded. Update your boss regularly on your progress and potential delays.

2. **Assignment Completion.**

   Tell your boss when you finish an assignment and ask for feedback. If you consistently ask for feedback, there should be no surprises at your performance review.

3. **Anticipated Problems.**

   If you anticipate a delay for any reason, inform your boss. Confront a problem at once so it does not escalate. Your boss may have ideas for how you can work around those problems. Do not cover up your mistakes. It is more difficult to explain why you hid the mistake than why you made it.

SUCCESSFUL EMPLOYEE ACTIONS (continued)

MONTHLY STATUS REPORT

Many employees have found that submitting a monthly status report is helpful in communicating problems. Although status reports take time, they are effective in keeping your boss informed and creating a record of what you have done, which can be helpful for performance evaluations or job interviews.

Exercise 2: Sample Monthly Status Report

Monthly Status Report

Name ____________________ Date __________

1. Completed Assignments:

A) ____________________

B) ____________________

C) ____________________

D) ____________________

2. Status on Current Projects:

A) ____________________

B) ____________________

C) ____________________

D) ____________________

3. Anticipated Problems or Concerns:

____

____

TURN COMPLAINTS INTO PROPOSALS

When you are reporting about a concern or problem, always be prepared with solutions. Bosses love to see initiative and problem-solving skills in their employees. This is a simple way to show what you can do. You may want to write your ideas down so your boss can read them. Written reports have two advantages: they put the decision-making back into the boss' lap and they can be given to a higher authority so you can receive credit for your ideas. Ask if your boss prefers a combination of oral and written reports.

Exercise 3: Turning Complaints Into Proposals

Turning negatives to positives demonstrates one of the star abilities: creativity. Think of a complaint that you would like your boss to take action on and use the following sample complaint proposal form to put your thoughts in writing.

Complaint Proposal Form

1. Problem Area: ____________________
2. Potential Causes: ____________________
3. Solutions: ____________________
4. Recommended Solution and Rationale: ____________________
5. Implementation Strategy (Who, When, Where): ____________________

   ____
6. Progress Checkpoint (date to check on strategy effectiveness):

   ____

   ____

PRAISING UPWARD

Bosses need to know they are doing a good job. Many studies indicate that feedback is the number one motivator, yet often upper level managers do not receive any more feedback than you do. Providing feedback effectively demonstrates your star abilities of communication and creativity.

If you want to praise your boss, keep it specific and sincere. The story is told of the employee who told his boss, ''You are the best boss a person could ever have. Every night I go home and tell my wife how great you are and how much I enjoy working for you.'' Nobody will believe that.

Praise Example

Your boss gives you a copy of the minutes from her management staff meeting. You might say *(be specific)*, ''Mary, I want to let you know how much I appreciate your providing me with a copy of your management staff meeting minutes. *(Be sincere)* I find it extremely helpful to know how my projects fit in with the larger departmental focus. By seeing the big picture, I can target the information I provide you. Thanks for keeping me so well informed.''

How much do you want to bet that Mary will continue to give her employee copies of her minutes? Praise encourages us to continue that same behavior.

THINGS BOSSES DON'T WANT

In addition to understanding what abilities and behaviors your employer and organization find desirable, it is just as important to know what is unacceptable.

Exercise 5: Undesirable Behavior

The following is a list of employee behaviors that many managers find unacceptable. Please check those that you believe are very important to avoid.

____ **1.** To embarrass, surprise or confront one's supervisor publicly

____ **2.** To say nothing or to complain to other people when angry, depressed, demoralized or confused about work

____ **3.** To gossip and spread unfound rumors

____ **4.** To attempt a "palace coup," that is, to attempt to remove the boss from his or her position

____ **5.** To engage in undercover sabotage and to demoralize others

____ **6.** To steal time, property, information or ideas

____ 7. Other (specify) ____________________________________

THINGS BOSSES DON'T WANT (continued)

Most people enjoy an opportunity to rate themselves so they can identify areas for self-improvement. The following survey will help you assess whether you do things that your boss or organization do not find acceptable.

Exercise 6: Assess Yourself

Respond by checking "yes" or "no." Be honest with yourself.

	Yes	No
1. Do you usually have difficulty making decisions at work?	☐	☐
2. Are most of your decisions good?	☐	☐
3. Are you willing to stay at work past regular quitting time if a job is not completed?	☐	☐
4. Do you follow your organization's rules and directives?	☐	☐
5. Do you complain rarely and then only to your immediate supervisor?	☐	☐
6. Are you willing to accept responsibility for your mistakes?	☐	☐
7. Do you work hard at getting along with other workers and supervisors?	☐	☐
8. Are you friendly yet task-oriented at work?	☐	☐
9. Do you try to do your best at work?	☐	☐
10. Do you tend to put things off and do them at the last minute?	☐	☐

Give yourself one point for a "no" response on questions 1 and 10, and one point for each "yes" response on items 2–9. Scores of 9 and 10 are outstanding. Most employers would be delighted to have you working for them. Scores of 7 or 8 are above average. Your boss should consider you a valuable employee. A little improvement and you could be outstanding. Scores of 4 to 6 are within the average range. You and your boss would benefit from collaborative communication. Scores under 4 are below average. You need major changes on your job, or a new one.

Once you have assessed any undesirable behaviors, you can make improvements.

Exercise 7: Make Improvements

List the most critical questions from Exercise 6. Describe why the questions you checked may be a problem, and list changes you wish to make. An example is provided.

ACTION EXAMPLE

Question Number	Reason and Action Steps
1	*Reason:* I have trouble making decisions because my boss changes her mind frequently. *Action:* Try to get written directions even if I write them. Then, check on progress frequently to be sure I am on track.

Question Number	Reason and Action Steps
________	*Reason:* ________ ________ *Action:* ________ ________
________	*Reason:* ________ ________ *Action:* ________ ________
________	*Reason:* ________ ________ *Action:* ________ ________

SECTION

VIII

Managing Time Management Monsters

All over the world, companies are merging and laying off employees. The problem for the remaining staff is how to get all the necessary work done. How do we cope with multiple priorities and multiple bosses? What do we do with a boss who is disorganized? Time is what we want the most and what we use the worst.

PRODUCTIVITY PRINCIPLES

Before you can build a solid partnership with your supervisor, you need to concentrate on some basic productivity principles. Some people claim that planning takes all the sport out of life—yet the key to managing time effectively is planning so that your goals come to fruition. Some claim that unless we invest 1% of each project's time-span on planning, the project will take 2.7 times longer to complete. We will now examine the basic steps of time management:

PLANNING STEPS

1. **Analyze the situation.** Set goals according to your own values and purpose, within the framework of the organization. Your goals should also meet your supervisor's goals. Set up a three-to-five year plan and break it down into achievable one year plans. Ask yourself, ''What do I need to do this year (month, week) to get closer to achieving my long-range goals?''

2. **Develop weekly objectives.** Establish short-range goals that will lead you to your long-range plans.

3. **Make decisions on priority items and develop a daily plan.** Prioritize according to your and the organization's goals. You may want to use an ABCD system (or whatever system works for you).

A	**=**	**Important (goal-related) and urgent**
B	**=**	**Important, but not urgent**
C	**=**	**Urgent, but not important**
D	**=**	**Neither important nor urgent**

Once you have come up with a list of what needs to be done, prioritize using your system, and estimate how long each item will take. Continually rearrange your schedule so that you do the most important things first; block out large chunks of time for the really important tasks.

Sometimes everything becomes an A priority, and we begin living from crisis to crisis. Do not do whatever screams the loudest unless it is important. Learn to say no. Focus on the B tasks, which will give the biggest payoff. Constantly remind yourself of your goals and ask yourself what you have done today to get one step closer to them.

4. **Stick to your plan and review the results.** It will probably take about thirty days of concentrated effort to get your plan to work for you. Most people who stick to it for several months really get hooked and cannot imagine what they did before they used it.

How to Manage the Monsters

Planning is not the only ingredient in effective time management. Many barriers can restrict effective time management in boss-employee partnerships.

BARRIER 1: INTERRUPTIONS

Generally, 80% of your interruptions come from 20% of the people. What if that 20% is your boss? Here are some ideas for limiting interruptions:

1. Hold bi-weekly meetings with your boss. Strategize ways to minimize your boss' interruptions.

2. Hold stand-up meetings. This eliminates unnecessary socializing. Do not sit down when you go into your boss's office for a quick question.

3. If your boss comes into your office frequently and takes up too much of your time, stand up immediately or maintain your working posture; i.e., keep your hands on the keyboard. Tell your boss diplomatically that this is not a good time to interrupt.

   Use interruption times to delegate upwards. Ask your boss for help. Do not ask them if they stopped by for a particular reason. That will merely prolong the interruption. If it was important, they will let you know.

4. Be assertive—learn to say ''no.'' It is particularly difficult to say no to your boss. It must be done with tact and diplomacy so that your behavior will not reflect negatively on your performance evaluation.

Saying No to Your Boss

Before you say no to your supervisor, make sure you are fully utilizing your support staff and other team members. Some people might not be as swamped as you are. Ask them for help. Develop support staff so that you can delegate more work. Then things can get done that need to be done even when you are not there.

When you say no to your boss:

- Acknowledge the boss' request. Be sure you understand it.
- Give the reason why you cannot; negotiate.
- Provide alternatives.

For example, if your boss asks you to photocopy a report, say that you would be happy to (acknowledge request), but you are at a critical step on project xyz (give reason). Should you stop working on project xyz, or could your boss wait for the copies until tomorrow (provide alternative)?

Negotiate with your boss. When you are asked to do something, determine first the resources (staff and money) that will available, the level of authority you will have, what kind of feedback you can expect and project deadlines. Once you have said no, anticipate that your boss will come back with a stronger plea for help. Refuse again with the same reason so that your manager senses your honesty and firmness about the situation.

BARRIER 1: INTERRUPTIONS (continued)

5. Rearrange your office so that you are not facing the open door and cannot catch people's eyes as they go by. Remove guest chairs.

6. Discuss with your boss the idea of establishing a quiet time—a known period where you accept no interruptions or phone calls. This is work time to be guarded preciously. It is very important for you to return phone calls and messages when using this system so that people do not feel compelled to interrupt you.

7. If you have your own office, close your door and post a sign that says, ''Please do not interrupt. I will be available at (time).'' Put a notepad on your door so people can leave messages.

If you are in an open space environment, use a flag system to let people know when you are not to be interrupted. A green flag means interrupt me if necessary, yellow is enter with caution and a red flag means enter only if an emergency.

8. Use team logs. Set up a sheet of paper or file folder for each key person you work with. When you think of something to ask them, ask yourself, ''Can this wait?'' If it can, enter it on their team log sheet. If it cannot wait, interrupt them. If your supervisor interrupts you, ask him/her the questions from your team log. At an agreed upon time, go over each other's team logs.

SAMPLE TEAM LOG:

Date ____________ **Name of Key Person** __________________________

—Confirm project meeting time frame and location

—Ask about new personnel policy application to our department

—Computer sales person desires meeting—interested?

—Luncheon meeting with client Smith is cancelled for next Tuesday

BARRIER 1: INTERRUPTIONS (continued)

9. Have visitors screened by a third party. Set up call-back periods and return all your calls at once.

10. Set time limits on meetings.

BARRIER 2: CHANGING PRIORITIES

When you do not know what your priorities are, or your boss changes priorities frequently, you may become frustrated and feel a lack of accomplishment from your job. There are a couple of things you can do.

When your boss changes priorities, ask ''How does this affect the course of direction we were on?'' If there are no priorities, develop a sense of what the priorities should be, based on your knowledge of the organization's goals and mission. Review your list, tell your boss what you are doing and ask for feedback. Be flexible. You may not see the big picture, so ask questions and seek feedback.

BARRIER 3: COPING WITH MULTIPLE BOSSES

Multiple bosses can mean multiple directives. What can you do?

Always ask your bosses for time frames and priority levels. Communicate immediately if there is a conflict. Let the bosses work out among themselves which is the most important task to complete. Offer alternatives when saying no. Alternatives include different time frames than those requested, suggestions for who else might be able to help out and where else the work might be handled. Ask the bosses to help you design a work order form, which will help you determine priorities, manage the work flow and lessen interruptions. Different colored paper could indicate the priority level of the requests.

SAMPLE WORK ORDER FORM

Today's date: ____________ Requested by: ____________

Time submitted: ____________

Project/Item: ____________

Return to me: ☐ Draft ☐ Final

Formatting space: ☐ Single ☐ Double ☐ Triple

Type of paper: ____________

No. of copies I need: ________

Send additional copies to the following: ____________

Mail: ☐ Overnight ☐ Certified ☐ Regular

☐ Hand Deliver ☐ FAX

Work completed by: ____________

Date: ____________ Time: ____________

As long as the requests are not confidential, you can stack these work order forms on your desk in priority order. Then it is easy to point out to your boss(es), when a new request is made, what you are working on and where the new request fits in.

BARRIER 4: LACK OF INFORMATION

Information is power and the lack of it greatly lessens your chance of doing an effective job. There are several ways you can try to gain access to information from your boss.

Tell your boss that you need the information. Be diplomatically aggressive—use meetings, the phone and memos to ask for the information. Be sincere. Share your feelings of frustration with your boss, and ask if there is anything you can do to get access to the information. Follow up when you do not hear from your boss. Put information items on the bi-weekly meeting agenda. Plan ahead for slow response time. Use electronic mail to facilitate information sharing. Ask for a copy of your boss' management staff meeting minutes so that you can get a better sense of the big picture.

Put your project recommendations in writing and give a deadline date: ''If I do not hear from you by (date), I will proceed as outlined.''

BARRIER 5: UNAVAILABLE BOSS

If your boss is never around, it means he or she trusts you. However, sometimes you need to see your boss. Take control and set time aside to meet.

Take your boss off-site, away from the telephone and other interruptions—the break room, a local restaurant or conference room might work. Never surprise your boss. Put things in writing, or use office technology including voice mail or electronic mail to leave and retrieve messages.

Build alliances with peers and secretaries. They may have more access to the boss and be willing to share information they have obtained. Discuss the problem with your boss and agree on a system to share information.

BARRIER 6: DISORGANIZED BOSS

Robert Half International surveyed executives and found they waste nearly four weeks a year because they cannot find things and another three weeks a year on unnecessary phone calls. So what can you do for your disorganized boss?

Keep a dated copy of everything you send to your boss. Help your boss establish realistic time frames. Be flexible and use your energy to help alleviate the problem rather than escalate it. Share your frustration and confront the issue. If you are an organized assistant or the secretary, screen phone calls and interruptions. Suggest a daily quiet time. Try to anticipate your employer's needs; plan ahead. Try to understand the external factors that may be influencing your boss' organizational style. Recognize the different personality styles and how they affect time usage. Determine how you might minimize your boss' weaknesses as well as your own.

A FINAL THOUGHT

Time is money. The only person who saves time is the one who spends it wisely in the first place. Better time management will help you and your boss become more time-effective partners.

SECTION

IX

Coping with Dreadful Bosses

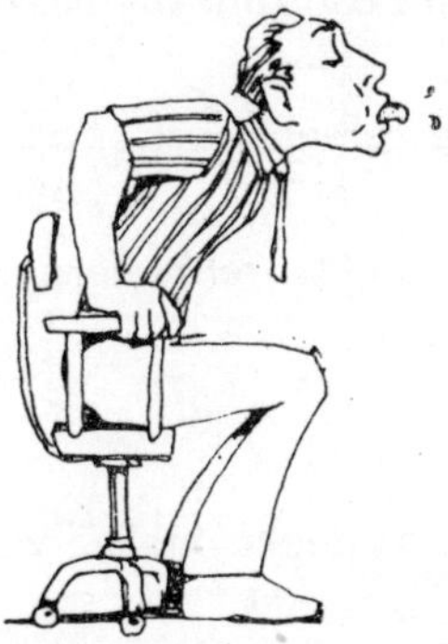

Graduate psychology student John Morrison of the University of Tulsa conducted a two-year study about why bosses are unpopular with their employees. The study, presented to the American Psychological Association and reported in the *APA Monitor,* revealed that:

- The most stressful job aspect for 60% of workers is their immediate supervisor.
- Many employees have spent a great deal of time working for what they consider a dreadful boss.

The researchers concluded from this study and others that 60%–75% of managers are incompetent.

ALL BOSSES ARE NOT CREATED EQUAL

Some bosses are a joy and a delight to work with. If you have one like this, count yourself blessed and give this person lots of positive feedback. However, even the best supervisor sometimes engages in problem behavior, especially when stress and tension are high.

A problem boss, on the other hand, can make life miserable for employees. Some workers "fire" their bosses and move on to other opportunities; others develop techniques and strategies to cope with dreadful bosses.

The qualities you bring to a professional relationship can help determine your relationship with your boss, including:

- Level of self esteem and job experience
- Willingness to take risks and confront the boss
- Flexibility to change jobs or careers
- Dependency on company benefits: retirement, medical, tuition credits, etc.
- Value system
- Sense of humor and ability to depersonalize work relationships
- Behavioral style
- Time and energy for improving the relationship with your boss
- Satisfaction with the work itself compared to the amount of stress in the relationship
- Degree of open communication with your boss

Because of our qualities, each of us will draw the line at a different point at what we consider to be dreadful. For example, one boss may be very demanding and tyrannical, but employees may find that he is also fair and honest. A person who has high self-esteem might not find this type of boss as difficult as someone who is sensitive and new to the job.

Choose A Boss!

INTOLERABLE BOSS BEHAVIOR

The first of the following two lists includes supervisory behaviors that some would find unacceptable. The second list includes strategies people have used to cope with them:

► **Personal Quirks**

This person may demonstrate exaggerated normal characteristics to the point of creating problems. For example, a commitment to quality work can lead to perfectionism; friendliness can lead to an exaggerated need to be liked, with consequent neglect of job tasks. Psychological problems such as depression, drug and alcohol abuse or mental disabilities can result in unpredictable behavior.

► **Slave-Driver Bosses**

A slave-driver supervisor may threaten, criticize and unreasonably demand work from employees. This boss may set unrealistically high expectations, not accept disagreement and use power and a biting tongue to dominate and manipulate employees.

► **Incompetent Bosses**

This boss cannot make a decision or may avoid contact with employees. This manager may cave in easily to pressure or change direction frequently and without warning. S/he does not know how to manage people.

The same boss may use a combination of intolerable behaviors and add a few twists. It is possible to have a slave driver boss who also has personal quirks. On the other hand, a quirky manager may be competent in all other ways.

An important criteria to use in determining unacceptable boss behavior is to consider the impact both on the individual employee and on the organization as a whole.

WHAT CAN YOU DO?

► **No Action**

Continue to do your work. Bottle up feelings and accept pain caused by negative and destructive supervisor. Take no action to improve the situation. Pause to observe and think before doing anything. *Taking no action will not put your job at risk, but it may greatly affect your productivity and health.*

► **Modify Your Own Behavior**

Adjust your work style to the needs of your boss. Use better communication strategies. Adapt your behavioral style to your boss' needs regarding use of time, level of detail, friendliness, change and perfectionism, etc. Change your responses (thoughts and feelings) to your boss' actions. This behavior has a *low to moderate risk regarding loss of job, but has higher potential for job improvement.*

► **Manage Your Boss**

Provide praise and criticism. Meet with your boss privately to improve the situation. Meet in a group to develop agreements. This behavior has a *moderate risk, because you must take the initiative. However, the potential for improvement is great.*

► **Oppose Your Boss**

Openly criticize or confront your supervisor's unacceptable behavior. Seek relief at the next level. Refuse to follow directives. Break company rules. This behavior exposes you to a *high risk of losing your job; however, it may be necessary when the effect of your boss' behavior is destructive.*

► **Fire Your Boss**

Transfer within the company. Quietly seek alternative employment and leave. Leave without another job. This behavior poses a *high risk to current employment and possibly to future employment. However, this step may become positive if done in a planned, rather than impulsive, manner.*

RISK TO ACTION STEPS DIAGRAM

The following diagram illustrates the relationship between level of risk and action steps. As the action steps move higher, the level of risk also rises.

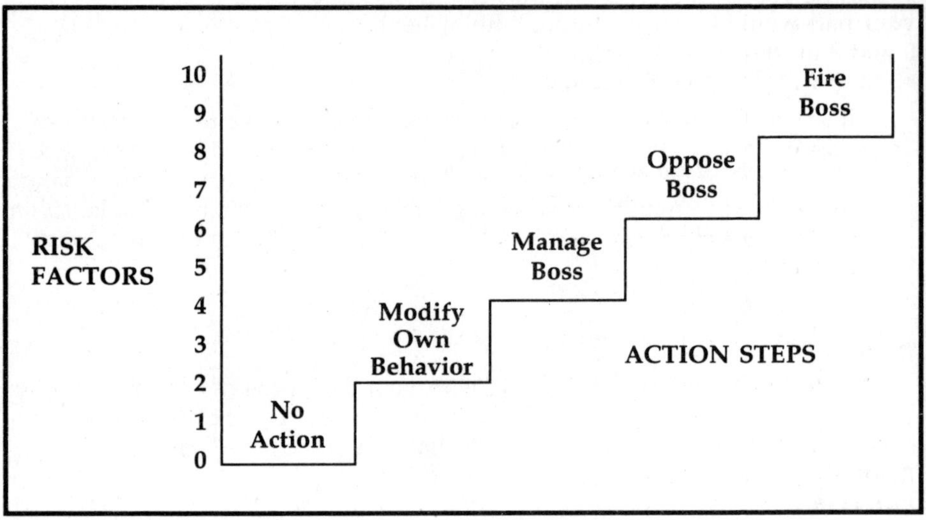

SCALE 1: Level of Risk

How do you know which strategy to match to which behavior? The choice is directly related to the level of risk you are willing to assume and how severe you perceive the problem to be.

Exercise 1: How Bad Is It Really?

Using the following scale, pinpoint your willingness to take risks. The descriptions next to the scale suggest what a person who exercises low, medium or high risk behavior might do. Make an *x* on the vertical line where you think your risk factors are. (For example, if you feel that any action on your part would endanger future employment, you will mark an *x* between 0 and 3 on the vertical line.)

	Scale	
	10	**High Risk:** Completely open and direct about what I feel and think. Unafraid of negative consequences. Know I can get a better job, probably with better pay. Do not feel locked in to benefits. Will leave if things get impossible.
	9	
	8	
	7	
RISK FACTORS	**6**	
	5	**Medium Risk:** Can raise some issues and discuss some feelings and ideas. Carefully choose the issues that I need to raise, but ignore others. Use some upward management techniques.
	4	
	3	
	2	
	1	**Low Risk:** Accept things as they are. Am very cautious about rocking the boat. Will not talk at all about my concerns for fear of retribution. Cannot risk losing job and benefits.
	0	

SCALE 2: Severity of Problem

This second scale reflects how much negative impact your boss' behavior has on you (and others') feelings and ability to work. The descriptions below the scale suggest what bosses do who create low, medium or high problems for their employees. Mark an *x* on the horizontal line where you believe the degree of problem severity falls.

PROBLEM SEVERITY

LOW										HIGH
0	**1**	**2**	**3**	**4**	**5**	**6**	**7**	**8**	**9**	**10**

Low Severity

Most of the time, my working relationship with my boss is satisfactory. Occasionally, when very stressed, she is disorganized, noncommunicative and sarcastic. It usually passes with time. Does not have serious impact.

Medium Severity

Boss is tough, very demanding and critical. Hard to please. Sometimes tries to improve by reading management books and taking courses. Has made some improvement. Affects me and other employees variously depending on the situation.

High Severity

Supervisor is unethical, rigid, emotionally disturbed, unfeeling. Impossible to do my job well because of poor information and constant criticism. Employees suffer from low morale, high turnover.

SCALE 3: Risk, Severity and Action Steps

The following scale illustrates the relationships between the level of risk you are willing to take (vertical line), the degree of severity of the boss's behavior (horizontal line) and the most appropriate strategies (stair steps).

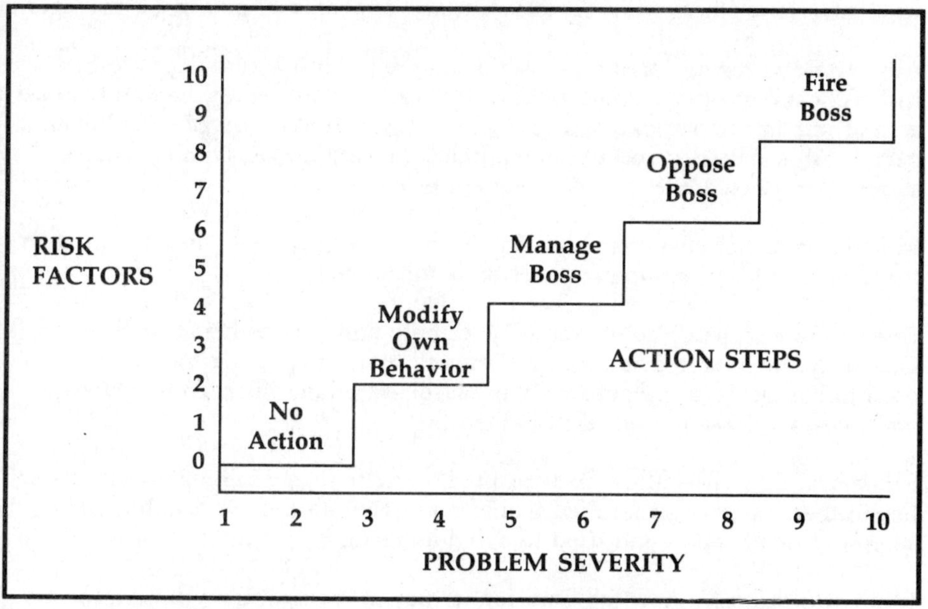

If the problem is very severe and a person is willing to take a high risk, the most successful action steps will be close to the top of the stair steps. You can increase your willingness to take risks by improving your work skills, getting more education or practicing more assertive communication. These actions will give you more confidence and employment options and you will be less fearful of losing this job.

Real-World Examples

The case studies on the following pages provide real-life examples of the relationships between employees' willingness to take risks, the supervisor's impact on employee's success and the types of steps taken in various scenarios.

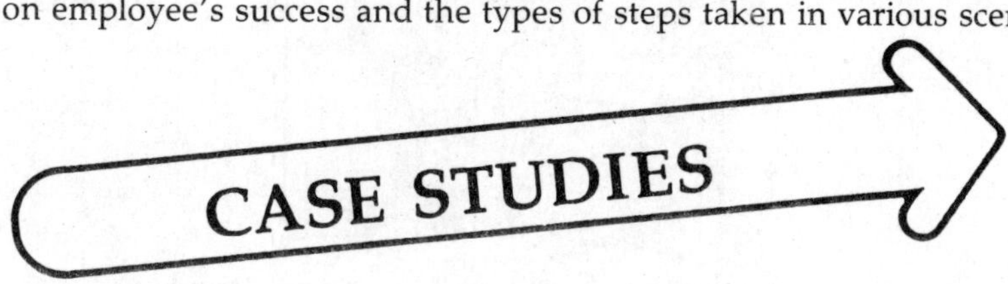

CASE STUDY 1: GOOD GUY/BAD GUY

Sarah left her job at a major university to work for a higher salary as a secretary for an architectural firm owned by two brothers. Fred, the owner who interviewed her, was very pleasant and appeared to be a good manager.

After working for one month, Sarah discovered that Ed, the older brother, had daily supervisory responsibilities. He was a tyrant who yelled and cursed at staff publicly and spoke demeaningly of them to other people. He hovered over Sarah's shoulder and reminded her to be careful. His continual close supervision caused her to make frequent errors.

In addition to her customary secretarial duties, both brothers had Sarah shop for family gifts and run personal errands for them.

One of the architects, Tom, was very friendly and supportive at first. Gradually, he started interrupting her work by talking to her too much. Sarah tried to handle Tom diplomatically because she valued his friendship in an otherwise unpleasant work environment.

Sarah had a good relationship with Fred, but she feared talking to him about his brother, assuming that Fred would disagree with her. So Sarah quietly accepted the situation and tried to avoid arousing Ed's anger.

Sarah was offered a new job with higher pay at the university where she used to work. To this day, Sarah omits her 6 month employment with the architects from her resume.

Exercise 2

Now we will assess the good guy/bad guy scenario.

1. On the risk scale from Exercise 1, where would you place Sarah? ________

   Why? ____

   ____

2. Where would you rate the degree of problem severity? ________

   Why? ____

   ____

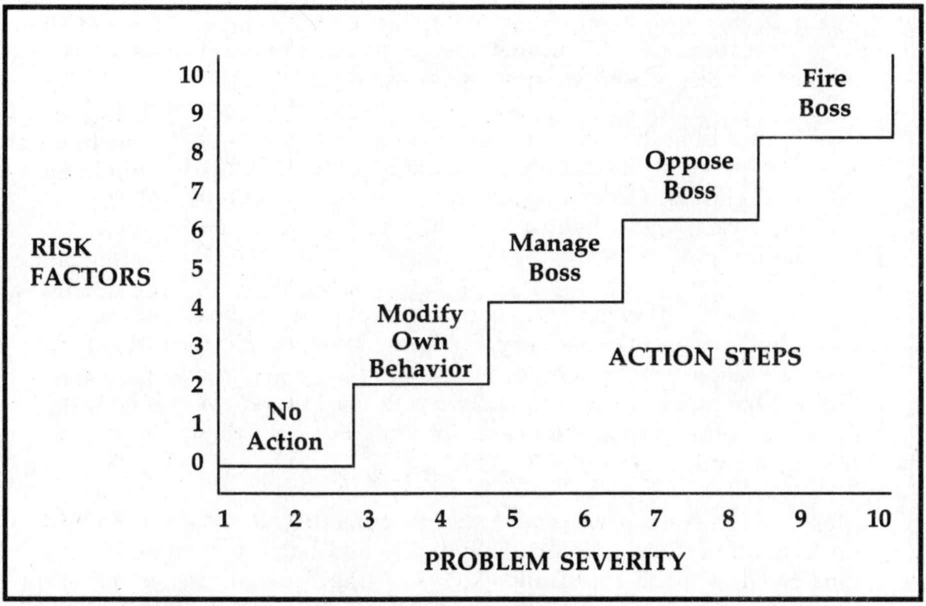

3. Do you believe Sarah handled her boss-employee relationship appropriately? ________ Why or why not? ____________________

   ____

4. What else could Sarah have done? ____________________

   ____

5. What would you have done in a similar situation? ____________________

   ____

AUTHOR'S ASSESSMENT OF CASE 1

Sarah initially chose a low-risk approach to her relationships with Ed, Fred and Tom: doing nothing. The overly friendly associate created more stress, particularly since she was not assertive with him. For Sarah, the situation was a medium to high risk problem severity, because she was fearful of her boss and it increased her error rate. She moved directly from doing nothing to firing her boss.

Sarah could have improved her situation by taking intermediate steps:

- Clarify her job duties through discussions with both owners and reopen these discussions as needed

- Give clear feedback to Tom that she appreciated his friendly support, but not the distractions from her work

- Change her thoughts and feelings about Ed's behavior. For example, when he yelled at her publicly, she might imagine him with a funny nose and glasses. Or, she could say to herself, "Everyone knows I'm a good secretary, and he just looks like a bad boss when he yells like this."

- Try to make Fred an ally. This step could be risky unless handled with great diplomacy. She could say, "When Ed yells at me for making mistakes, especially with other people around, it gets me so nervous that I make more errors. I'm really trying hard to get everything done right. The other day a client came in while Ed was yelling and it was very awkward.

  "It would help me if you could suggest something I can do to improve my communications with Ed. I think it would help everyone if he didn't yell so much because it's so distracting. It must also be stressful for him. His face gets red and you can see his veins pop out."

CASE STUDY 2: THE BOTTLENECK BOSS

When Bob became executive director for a metropolitan social services agency, the finances were in bad shape and staff could not keep up with the requests for services. Bob moved in enthusiastically. He was committed to keeping informed and checking on the work of his 500 employees. No one could accuse Bob of laziness. He started work early and left late. When he walked down the hall, everyone trembled, for fear he would bring them one of their mistakes with a lecture about being careful.

When a series of news articles criticized Bob for his management methods and the problems that were apparently caused by employees, he asked everyone to sign a loyalty oath. He insisted on reviewing every letter that went out to be sure it was perfect. He made it clear that no one could be trusted.

Sue, one of the department managers, had an increasingly difficult time with Bob's suspiciousness and checking compulsion. Paperwork got bottlenecked in Bob's office; personnel found themselves waiting indefinitely for decisions.

Sue liked her job, felt well paid, but knew she needed to take some calculated risks before her department's work slowed to a crawl. So, Sue did a boss analysis. She tried to see his perspective, listed his goals and looked at his behavioral style. Then, she assessed how serious the problem was and decided she could manage a medium-high risk. However, she wanted to start at the lowest risk level that would bring positive results.

CASE STUDY 2 CONTINUED

CASE 2: THE BOTTLENECK BOSS (continued)

The following scale reflects Sue's decisions:

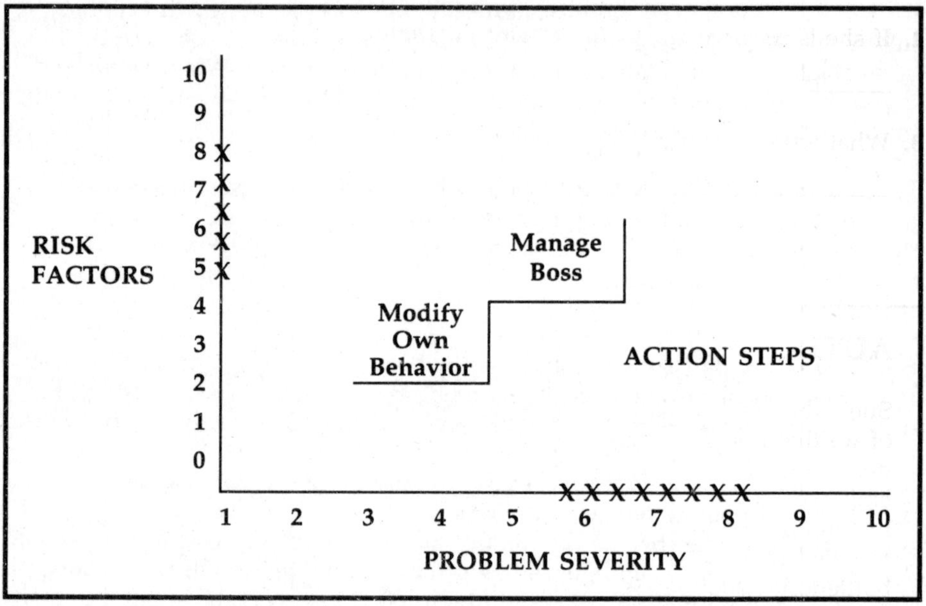

It was apparent to Sue that Bob was a perfectionist and his style became exaggerated under stress. Bob felt stressed by the newspaper articles, so he was suspicious and distrustful.

Sue laid out and followed several strategies over a six-month period:

- Provide lots of written and oral information
- Ask his opinion on the best way to speed up the process; explain the consequences of delayed paperwork
- Whenever possible, give him positive feedback about the improvements in the agency's finances and accuracy of record keeping
- Demonstrate loyalty to him by making him look good in public
- Avoid a power push

Exercise 3

Now assess the bottleneck boss.

1. What do you believe will be the likely outcome of Sue's efforts? ________

____

2. If she is unsuccessful, what else could she do? ________

____

3. What would you do if you worked for a boss like this? ________

____

AUTHOR'S ASSESSMENT OF CASE 2

Sue's thoughtful approach is likely to be successful if she has the luxury of waiting for Bob to move faster while the rest of the agency slows down and waits for him. She might suggest that her peers and employees follow the same strategy. Together, they increase the potential for improvement if they keep Bob's paranoia under control and get him to delegate more responsibility. If Bob continues to engage in his bottleneck actions, Sue might need to escalate her risk quotient with more direct and possibly confrontational steps. Working in an agency under public censure could affect her future career. Sue might set a mental time line to find another position if the situation worsens.

S E C T I O N

X

Chutes or Ladders

Most people are interested in climbing the career ladder and prefer not to slip down the ''chute'' to an untimely and involuntary employment exit. Employees who feel most successful have learned how to achieve their own goals (security, recognition, autonomy) while contributing to the company's success.

ASSESS YOURSELF

Both you and your supervisor are responsible for assessing how your performance contributes to your mutual success. The following self-assessment scoresheet will pinpoint areas for improvement and help you figure out whether you will stagnate or surge ahead in your career.

Many of the strategies will help protect your career from the ravages of a dreadful supervisor. For example, by building skills, reputation and support networks, you will have more flexibility to take risks.

Exercise 1: Your Career Advancement Scoresheet

Rate the frequency with which you perform the following activities. Use the rating scale: 5 = always; 4 = most of the time; 3 = sometimes; 2 = rarely; 1 = never.

	Score
1. Attend work-related conferences when available	_____
2. Advise decision makers of my interest in advancement, according to procedures and customs of the organization	_____
3. Participate in meetings or other group activities	_____
4. Receive positive feedback from others without asking for it	_____
5. Speak positively about my company to outside people	_____
6. Keep informed of requirements for career advancement in my company and field	_____
7. Read items in my specialty to keep up-to-date	_____
8. Read outside my field to learn new skills	_____
9. Attend seminars, courses, speeches to expand skills	_____
10. Observe the unwritten rules of my organization such as dress code, behavioral styles and friendship patterns	_____

	Score
11. Seek increased responsibilities such as serving on committees, project teams, etc.	_____
12. Belong to at least one work-related organization such as a trade association	_____
13. Serve on a committee of at least one community or professional organization	_____
14. Talk to friends and relatives about my career plans	_____
15. Expand my circle of acquaintances to include people who can help me with career advancement	_____
16. Complete assignments on time	_____
17. Go the extra mile to satisfy customers	_____
18. Receive above average to excellent evaluations	_____
19. Adhere to policies and procedures of company	_____
20. Make changes or suggest ways to improve work	_____
21. Perform work well	_____
22. Maintain exemplary attendance records	_____
23. Communicate clearly	_____
24. Seek feedback on the quality of my work	_____
25. Work on aspects of my performance that need improvement	_____
26. Develop and implement personal career plans based on an annual self-assessment	_____
27. Be known as a self-starter	_____
28. Display a positive attitude	_____

CAREER ADVANCEMENT SCORESHEET (continued)

	Score
29. Get along well with peers, supervisors, clients and others	______
30. If I have a personal conflict, find ways to resolve it	______

SCORING YOURSELF: Add your responses and compare your score with the table below.

Very Low	1–30
Low	31–60
Medium	61–90
High	91–120
Very High	121 and above

Very low scores indicate you are not moving ahead. You may believe many of the career myths including the one that people get ahead by just doing their work and minding their own business. Perhaps you feel you do not have enough time for the ''extras'' such as reading.

Low scores suggest that you have developed career skills in some areas but not in others. Identify where you need to improve. Is shyness holding you back from promoting yourself?

Medium scores imply that you are not overly fearful of reaching for success. Sharpen your career goals and continue to use self-promotion techniques.

High scores indicate self-confidence and ambition. You have excellent prognosis for success. You know what your goal is and how to reach it.

Very high scores suggest that you are probably already reaping career success. You need to guard against over-confidence and brashness so you do not offend others. Keep your performance quality high and be considerate of people around you.

EVALUATING YOUR SCORESHEET

Quality work is essential, but it is not the sole prerequisite for career success. The right people must be aware of your work and how you contribute to the organization.

High visibility can be a double-edged sword, however, advertising both strengths and weaknesses. A good barometer of your image is whether or not you receive unsolicited compliments and recognition, particularly from superiors.

If you need to raise your positive image, explore techniques that feel natural. Contribute a new idea or solution to a problem; offer assistance or say thank you to others.

To expand your flexibility and options, commit yourself to a life-long program of education. Today's workplace is in the midst of an information revolution. The pressure to update your knowledge and skills comes from all sides: the impact of computers, a constant influx of well-trained employees and the increasing number of job seekers. Read, take classes and observe your co-workers. Expand your horizons into related or new fields.

Observe the unwritten rules of your firm. Do not violate your company's codes unless you want negative publicity. For example, pay attention to the dress code, interpersonal forms of address and subtle requirements for overtime. A warning light should flash in your mind if your value system conflicts with your company's customs and philosophy.

Successful employment is a contact game. You need personal associations within and outside your work place. A supportive circle of associates and friends provides information. But all the visibility and contacts in the world will be purposeless unless the quality of your work is satisfactory. Find out what your job requires. Develop your skills, then make the extra effort to achieve excellence.

ASSESS YOURSELF (continued)

Exercise 2: Your Self-Improvement Action Plan

Your scores in the career advancement scoresheet may suggest areas of your career that need more attention. The scoresheet is divided into five groupings: *visibility* (questions 1–5), *education* (questions 6–10), *contacts* (questions 11–15), *work quality* (questions 16–25), and *personal* (questions 26–30).

Review the statements in each of the five groups to develop your own action plan. Examples are provided as thought starters.

A. VISIBILITY (#1–5)

Example: "I will attend the next annual meeting of the Society of Internal Auditors."

Insert your action plan to improve *visibility.*

____

B. EDUCATION (#6–11)

Example: "I will subscribe to *Harvard Business Review* and read articles on finance."

Insert your action plan to improve *education.*

____

C. CONTACTS (#11–15)

Example: "Next week, I will ask Bill to add me to the communications task force."

Insert your action plan to improve *contacts.*

____

D. WORK QUALITY (#16–25)

Example: "The idea I have to reduce paperwork needs to be tested. I'll discuss it with Betty at our next supervisory meeting."

Insert your action plan to improve *work quality.*

____

E. PERSONAL (#26–30)

Example: "I will let Ed know that his frequent interruptions are making it very hard for me to get his work done on time."

Insert your action plan to improve *personal.*

____

HOW TO ACHIEVE GOOD PERFORMANCE EVALUATIONS

For most people the performance evaluation process is extremely painful. It has traditionally been used as a time to report bad news to the individual, such as all the mistakes made during the past year. Not only is it personally painful to hear criticism, but the evaluation process is often tied to salary adjustments for the coming year.

More enlightened organizations and their managers are learning how to give feedback regularly and to use the periodic, formal evaluation as opportunity to summarize feedback already provided as well as to set annual goals.

Whether or not your organization does this, you can take several steps to assure that your performance evaluation is fair, accurate and positive.

STEP 1: Set Performance Goals

Before anyone can measure anything, there must be a standard against which it can be compared. Prioritize your goals and discuss them with your boss. You may wish to include personal goals such as completing a degree or developing a new skill. Quantify your goals and always have someone else proofread them.

Depending upon your level of communication with your manager, you may choose to share your personal goals. Obviously, if you are interested in a promotion, your boss may be able to clarify what it requires.

Exercise 3: Goals Worksheet

Modify the following worksheet format to meet your needs:

My organizational goals for (dates) **to** **are:**

Goals	*Measurable Results*
1. ______	______
2. ______	______
3. ______	______

My personal goals for (dates) **to** **are:**

Goals	*Measurable Results*
1. ______	______
2. ______	______
3. ______	______

HOW TO ACHIEVE GOOD PERFORMANCE EVALUATIONS (continued)

STEP 2: Keep Score All Year Long

Bosses like to be kept informed about your progress toward your goals. By keeping records of achievements and problems, you can keep your supervisor informed, keep yourself on track and have documentation to support the formal performance evaluation.

Exercise 4: Achievement Record

Records provide specific information that is directly related to the agreed-upon organizational goals. Modify the following worksheet as needed:

Goal #	Evidence of Achievement	Evidence of Problems
1.	______________________	______________________
2.	______________________	______________________
3.	______________________	______________________
4.	______________________	______________________

STEP 3: Become a Partner in Your Performance Evaluation

You can prepare for the formal performance evaluation. Ask your boss for a meeting. Express your desire to be a productive employee. Say you want to discuss company expectations and your goals. Offer to show your boss your achievement records. Ask for specifics.

Handling Negative Feedback

Many employees find it more difficult to accept criticism than compliments from their boss. But the truly successful professional needs to know how to improve.

CRITICISM EXERCISE

Exercise 5: How Do I Handle Criticism?

1. Place a "plus" (+) by those situations you feel you handle appropriately; a "minus" (–) by those situations you avoid handling; and a "zero" (0) by those you may handle, but they cause internal stress or anxiety.

______ In a department meeting you make an important statement that everyone ignores.

______ Your boss criticizes your job performance.

______ Your boss makes a negative remark about your new haircut.

______ You hear from a colleague that your boss is upset about a comment you made in yesterday's staff meeting.

______ Your boss criticizes you unjustifiably.

______ At lunch, a manager makes a negative comment about a project you are in charge of.

______ You are depressed and your boss criticizes you for your bad attitude.

______ A manager from another department sends you a memo criticizing your latest idea.

______ You complete an assignment to the best of your ability and are told that you could have done a better job.

______ You ask your boss to consider you for leadership responsibilities on an exciting new project and are turned down.

2. In the situations that you marked with a plus, list the actions you take that cause you to be effective:

____

____

____

3. Analyze those situations you marked with a minus and a zero. Write down why those situations are difficult for you to handle and the actions you typically take:

A. Why Difficult?	B. Typical Response
______________	______________
______________	______________
______________	______________
______________	______________

Types of Criticism

The three types of criticism that you might experience are unjustified criticism, criticism that is vague or a difference of opinion, and valid criticism.

Unjustified criticism may come as a result of not living up to the fantasy our boss has created for us. Often, bosses do not tell us their expectations. For criticism to be helpful, we must ask for specific, concrete objectives so we can understand our boss' expectations and take action if we choose.

Vague criticism may indicate a difference of opinion. Your boss may think other values and methods of doing something are better than yours.

Valid criticism is the most difficult type of criticism for us to handle because we have to admit we are wrong. We tend to give more meaning to our mistake than necessary, to make it more important than it is. We must recognize that we all make mistakes. The more active and fruitful our lives, the more we will receive criticism.

Coping with Criticism from Our Boss

Once the criticism is made, the receiver has control of the next step. It is up to us to decide whether we believe the criticism has merit and is worth acting upon.

There are basically three stages you go through when handling criticism: *awareness, assessment and action.*

In the awareness stage, your natural instincts take over. You usually respond by counterattacking defensively or accepting the criticism silently at face value.

In the assessment stage you consider how the criticism was delivered, the intention of your boss, and how valid you believe the criticism to be. In the final stage, you decide on any action you want to take in response to the criticism.

If you can be assertive when being criticized, you will remain confident and cool during the process. An assertive approach strives to maintain a win-win attitude in which you allow your boss to have an opinion while maintaining your self-esteem.

RESPONDING TO UNJUSTIFIED CRITICISM

The first thing you must do when your supervisor criticizes you unjustifiably is to set a psychological barrier so that you do not take the criticism personally. One of the basic foundations for handling criticism effectively is self-confidence.

You must be good at what you do and believe in yourself or you will most likely crumble under your boss' criticism. If you believe in yourself, your abilities, skills and knowledge, criticism is much less threatening, and you will be able to take it less personally. You must choose to let the criticism have no impact. Do not countercriticize or countermanipulate or, worse yet, talk behind your manager's back.

FOGGING

When faced with unjustified criticism, "fog" the situation. Fogging is acknowledging the possibility that the criticism may contain some truth. Say, for example: "You could be right about . . . ," "You might be right about . . . ," "Perhaps I could . . . ," "Maybe I should . . .," "What you say makes some sense . . ." or "I'll consider your input. . . ."

If your boss criticizes how you handled a customer, say, "Perhaps I could have been more effective." Then ask for specifics on what to do differently. This way you merely acknowledge that perhaps you could have been more effective (we can always improve), which satisfies the critic.

REQUEST SPECIFIC FEEDBACK

This example incorporates a second technique, requesting specific feedback, which is very effective with vague criticism. This technique uses questions to focus on the future instead of dwelling on the error. It moves you directly into the action stage. Following is a list of responses you can use to get specific feedback.

- "What specifically did I do that . . ."
- "If you were in my shoes, what would you do differently?"
- "I'm not sure I understand what you mean. Can you please give me some examples of where I have done that?"
- "Is that all you can think of that I could do to improve my performance?"

A companion technique to requesting specific feedback is called the ECHO technique. It will help you listen more effectively and gain information from your boss that you can use to rectify the problem. You simply repeat the last three to six words of your critic.

RESPONDING TO UNJUSTIFIED CRITICISM (continued)

Case Scenario

Boss: "I'm not pleased with how this report looks. Please take another crack at it."

You: "What specifically do you not like about the report?"

Boss: "I don't like the format of the report."

You: "The format of the report?"

Boss: "Yes, the format. It seems a bit jumbled in places."

You: "A bit jumbled in places?"

Boss: "Yes . . . particularly on the third page."

You: "The third page?"

Boss: "Well, if you would rearrange the statistics with the text on page three, I think it would be easier to read."

You: "So, if I rearrange the statistics with the text on page three, the report would look better?"

Boss: "Yes."

You: "Is there anything else I should do differently with this report to make it more readable?"

ADMIT THE TRUTH

The last technique is the simplest and most effective when coping with valid criticism: admit the truth. You made a mistake, so admit it rather than making excuses, overapologizing or overcompensating for your error.

Sample Responses

"You're right. I didn't make my sales quota this month and this is what I'm planning to do to meet the quota next month . . ."

"That's right. I didn't use the correct formula when I was analyzing the numbers. I'll rework the report using the correct figures, now that I know them. Thanks for your feedback."

"You're right. I probably could have thought that through more carefully. What would you have done?"

Valid Criticism Scenario

Boss: "I think you could've handled the staff meeting more effectively this morning."

You: "I wasn't happy with how things went either. Next staff meeting, I'm planning to send an agenda out in advance so we can all be better prepared and use the time effectively. Do you have any other ideas on how I could make the meeting more effective?"

Exercise 6: Putting Your Skills to the Test

Now practice your skills in handling criticism. Use a combination of the fogging, requesting specific feedback/echo and admit the truth techniques. Write your answers on the lines provided.

1. Things haven't been going well for you lately, you are feeling a bit "down." Your boss says to you, "What's been bugging you lately . . . you sure have a bad attitude."

____

____

____

____

2. You have just completed an assignment. Your boss looks over it and comments to you, "I really had expected more from you as a senior professional in our group."

____

____

____

____

3. You hear from a colleague that your boss is upset about a comment you made in yesterday's staff meeting. You would like to "clear the air" with your boss.

____

____

____

____

VALID CRITICISM SCENARIO (continued)

Potential Responses to Situations 1–3 (from page 113)

1. "Perhaps I have been a bit down lately (fogging). Has this caused a problem in my performance that I have been unaware of?" (request specific feedback)

2. "What specifically had you expected from me as a senior professional in this group?" or "What would you have done differently?" (requesting specific feedback)

3. "I sense you were upset about the staff meeting yesterday. Was there anything that I said or did that is bothering you?" (request specific feedback)

SECTION XI

The Final Episode

You have now completed the book and you should be closer to an effective working partnership. It is your right and responsibility to manage your manager. It is part of your job.

THE FINAL EPISODE (continued)

You have the most vested interest in your career, personal satisfaction and happiness. These ideas will help you understand and focus on the big picture, communicate for greater impact and build bridges with your boss. You now know how to confront your supervisor with compassion and have analyzed your boss' behavioral style. You have learned how to manage those time management monsters and how to build your career ladder. The rest is up to you.

You really have three choices when it comes to your relationship with your manager:

1. **Change your manager**

2. **Change your environment**

3. **Change yourself**

Of these three choices, you have control over only yourself. So, what action are you going to take as a result of reading this book?

If you have already changed the way you cope with your boss, you may have experienced some of these benefits:

- Reduced physical and mental stress
- Increased opportunity for recognition and promotion
- The company implemented my ideas
- Increase in my self-confidence, motivation and morale
- Increased respect from colleagues
- Helped me make a career decision about whether to leave job
- Anticipate and avoid problems with my boss
- Improved the quality and quantity of work
- Increased enjoyment of my job

If you do not take action, not much will change.

We hope this book has helped you accept the things you cannot change in your job, has given you the courage to change the things you can, and that you have gained some knowledge in understanding the difference between the two.

Best wishes as you design your partnership plan and turn it into positive action!

ABOUT THE AUTHORS:

Patti Hathaway, M.A., is a results-oriented speaker, trainer and corporate consultant. She brings a fresh, dynamic approach based on the business savvy and insights gained from training over 13,000 people in 28 states since starting her business in 1987.

A highly rated trainer with Fred Pryor Seminars, Patti was selected as the State of Ohio's 1988 ''Outstanding Young Career Woman'' by the Business and Professional Women's Association (BPW). Patti is an active member of the National Speakers Association and has served on the board of directors of the Ohio Speakers Forum, Central Ohio ASTD, Capitol City BPW and Calvin College Alumni Association.

Susan D. Schubert, M.A., is a highly-experienced professional trainer, consultant and speaker. Satisfied clients value her ability to identify needs, formulate an action plan to meet those needs and accomplish it with grace and good humor. Her mark of distinction is a zealous and sensitive approach to participant involvement. Since starting her firm in 1983, she has worked with more than 250 companies, agencies, government entities and associations.

Susan is an officer of the Ohio Speakers Forum, member of the National Speakers Association, Central Ohio ASTD, active alumna of the Columbus Area Leadership Program and member of its affiliated National Management Association.

Susan and Patti invite your questions and ideas. Please contact them:

Patti Hathaway
The Change Agent
1016 Woodglen Road
Westerville, OH 43081
1-800-339-0973
www.thechangeagent.com
E-mail: patti@thechangeagent.com

Susan Schubert
Schubert-Kravitz Associates
7729 Eagle Creek Drive
Pickerington, OH 43147
1-800-686-8477
E-mail: SusanSays@aol.com

NOTES

NOTES